IMPROVISATION

By Mildred Portney Chase

JUST BEING AT THE PIANO

IMPROVISATION
Music From The Inside Out

Mildred Portney Chase

CREATIVE ARTS BOOK COMPANY
BERKELEY • 1988

For information contact:
    Creative Arts Book Company
    833 Bancroft Way
    Berkeley, CA 94710

Typography: QuadraType, San Francisco
Cover Design: Charles Fuhrman
Cover Art: C. W. Bergmüller

Library of Congress Cataloging-in-Publication Data

Chase, Mildred Portney.
  Improvisation: music from the inside out.

  Bibliography: p.
  1. Improvisation (music) 2. Piano—instruction and study.
I. Title.
MT68.C525 1988   781.6'5   87-30472
ISBN 0-88739-058-7 (pbk.)

Printed in the United States of America.

ACKNOWLEDGMENTS

I WISH TO express my deep appreciation for Don Ellis of Creative Arts Book Company for his response to and interest in publishing this book. His encouragement throughout the project meant much to me, inspiring my best efforts.

I could not have wished to work with a more sympathetic editor than Joan Minkler Harrison. Due to her fine music background, she was well equipped to make the best of the original manuscript.

Along with my appreciation for Don Ellis' sense of idealism, and the editor's dedicated efforts, I wish to express my indebtedness to the influences of my teachers, Victor Trerice, Mary Carr Moore, Olga Steeb, Josef Lhevinne, Rosina Lhevinne, Richard Buhlig, and Josef Rosenfeld. I should add the following names: Louis Persinger, Albert Spaulding, Felix Salmond, Carl Friedberg, and Alexander Siloti. The years at Juilliard were filled with working experiences with these great musicians without necessarily being their student; through chamber music, hearing them play and teach, and by osmosis. Add to these all the inspiring performances I have heard through the years and the words of wisdom shared through the written works by artists and thinkers of the highest standing. I have been fortunate to have had many people in my life; family and friends as well as students of all levels who have rekindled my idealism through the years.

M. C.

DEDICATION

I WISH TO dedicate this book particularly to the little people in my life, with whom it has been my privilege to make music; Jake, Ben, Zeke, Meredith, Kate, Ann, Oliver, Thea, Columbine, Michael, Aaron, Pia, Shivani, Christopher William, Michael Joseph, Ryan, Justin, Colin, Taralia and Julio. I have great hopes that music will continue to be one of the ways through which they will bring more joy and meaning to their own lives as well as to the others around them.

In
loving memory
of
William Francis Chase

The instinctive progressive interest of every man in art . . . will go on and on, ever fulfilling hopes, ever building new ones, ever opening new horizons, until the day will come when every man while digging his potatoes will breathe his own epics, his own symphonies. . . .

CHARLES IVES

CONTENTS

INTRODUCTION

I HAD NOT planned to write a book on improvisation. How could one put into words the thoughts and feelings about a process which is so transitory and personal? It was only after declining an invitation to write a magazine article on the subject that I realized a book was beginning to take shape. No sooner had I rejected the idea of writing about this subject than thoughts and feelings began to surface, urging me to write. Hesitantly at first, then gradually picking up momentum, sections began to form. I found myself talking back to books I was reading. Ideas began to stimulate new ideas. Other ideas were stimulated by the needs of students in the process of unfolding their abilities, the results generously rewarding me for the meager help I could offer. At times a mere suggestion was all it took. I felt the urge to share the joy of watching a student begin to improvise seemingly without effort.

This book reflects my convictions regarding the importance of improvisation in the development of musical abilities. It also expresses my deep belief that everyone has vast creative ability which needs only to be activated and nurtured.

To improvise is natural and intuitive, whereas not to improvise implies restriction and limitation. Very early in life we are allowed to learn to stand and take our first few steps before actually being told how to use our feet. We learn to speak before being told what words to use and how to arrange them in sentences. The baby is not stopped from repeating "ga ga ga ga ga" in the process of learning to speak, nor is it told to open the hand first and then close it around an object it seeks to grasp. Here the child is allowed to learn through intuitive exploration. Unfortunately, too often this intuitive exploring stops where formal "education" steps in. A common experience shared by too many students of music is that improvisation was either totally left out of their training, or it was simply ignored and in some instances was positively discouraged by parents or teachers. As a result, there are a great many performers, teachers and even composers who have never improvised. The effect of this deplorable omission as well as the ease with which it can be restored to its rightful place in anyone's musical experience are factors that inspired much of the content of this book.

The educational system encourages elitism in music by eliminating it from the essential curriculum, thus depriving those children who otherwise cannot afford it, and leaving the privilege to those children who are already well off. Our teaching institutions are known for moving slowly and ponderously like giant monsters with limited maneuverability and limited foresight. When they move it is with great caution and an air of superiority. Often influenced in strange ways and always seeking to save money, these institutions have cut the "nonessential" subjects such as music and art practically to the bone. At the same time, great expense goes towards constant testing and evaluating, which do not encourage children to learn or to discover but which only satisfy requirements for accountability and achievement. The result of this testing is that in many instances the "gifted" student may acquire an unrealistic self-image while the slower child is left behind at a rate increased by his self-consciousness and low self-esteem. The same time spent on testing and much of this so-called teaching could elicit better results in accountability and achievement were there more space and time for exploring within and around the knowledge and ideas presented. (It might be noted here that Albert Einstein was known to improvise at the piano on a daily basis, especially during periods of work on serious projects. Who is to say at which point this creative mind switched tracks from the musical to the scientific as he continued working through problems of wide-reaching effect? Who knows what ideas may be sown in such sessions that light the way to the subconscious mind, where intuition constantly lends herself to our every effort?) We may yet benefit from our gifts if we can connect with this nucleus of thought and action within the human being.

Improvisation could be described as the imagination guiding an action in an unplanned way, allowing a multitude of split second adjustments. We improvise in all areas of our lives every day. In speaking, for example, we improvise constantly. We may not have a definite idea in mind, yet the words seem to form themselves, choosing their own order. The moment we are concerned with grammar or logic we immediately become constrained and our speech will reflect that. These same conditions apply to the language of music, only here we invent new vocabulary as we go. Simply giving ourselves permission to play what we seem to hear in our minds or what our fingers mindlessly find for us, intuitively led, is really all that is required to release our ability to improvise.

In many instances, great potential in a student has been stifled and the creative muscles of the imagination have become atrophied. Many people develop a positive embarrassment associated with being creative. There are too many highly educated people who have never really tapped into their own creativity. Along with their other learning, they have acquired a sense of conviction that they really are without this ability. We are all vulnerable to this in varying degrees. The fortunate thing is that the ability to improvise lies within each of us and it only takes a reversal of thought to begin to bring it to use.

Once a student has begun improvising, and once the barriers of self-doubt and self-consciousness have been broken down, the gap between the level of improvising and that of already acquired playing skills is easily bridged, regardless of the student's age or degree of experience. It is not so much a matter of progressing over time as it is one of opening a gate with ready skills waiting to surge into activity. As a teacher, my role is often quite a passive one, but I have been impressed on too many occasions by real success for me to believe this ability to belong exclusively to the "talented."

The general discussions in this book are interspersed with examples of procedures and musical illustrations for potential use. Hopefully, these examples will serve as openers and eventually give way to the reader's inventiveness. Regardless of the amount of experience you may have with an instrument, you can make use of any of the exercises described. The process is not linear, requiring steps that are to be taken in a specific order. You may start in the middle and work your way backwards. The exercises and suggestions are not graded; the gradation is for each individual to realize. An exercise suggested for a child beginner will become a horse of a different color in the hands of an experienced adult. Consider the examples as gateways to open creative areas, and feel free to depart from the structure at any time if you find yourself drawn to exploring. They can serve as springboards for your own ideas. Different people using the same example can produce music so diverse that it is hard to believe it was rooted in the same soil. A small kernel of an idea can stimulate a forest of growth.

This book does not pretend to cover the subject completely—no one book could. Many things have been left unwritten, many aspects not outlined or just touched upon lightly. The field of electronics is not discussed here simply because it lies outside of my experience and qualifications. Also, specific instruction with regard to harmony and theory has been excluded for the most part, as the reader can find this in the many good harmony books available. The main intent of this book is to activate an appetite for experiencing music through musical inventiveness.

In his fine book, *Music Improvisation*, Derek Bailey suggests that one cannot learn to improvise from a book, and that in fact it cannot be taught. He maintains that improvisation is a skill that is acquired by "stumbling on the right method" through successful and unsuccessful experimentation. Nothing in my book is intended to serve as a method. Caution aside, I have persistently expressed my thoughts. There will undoubtedly be too many words in some places and not enough in others. However, despite the necessary incompleteness of my task, the attempt to bring improvisation into each person's musical experience should continue. While a number of references to other books on the subject are mentioned, there is still room for much more discussion. Hopefully, there will be enough additional contributions highlighting the subject of improvisation for the process to be completely dusted off and returned to its rightful place after having been practically eradicated from music training for the better part of a century. The whole experience should allow interaction between networks of awakened sensibilities and skills, each merging with the other, yet functioning independently. Hopefully, the interested reader will gain back some of the lost trust in his innate abilities and bring improvisation into the sphere of his musical experience.

CREATIVITY FOR SURVIVAL IN A COMPUTERIZED SOCIETY

WE LIVE IN a society in which we are constantly bombarded by the appearance of new scientific products at a pace that often makes yesterday's new items obsolete. All sorts of knowledge is being imprinted on miniature cuneiform tablets of the future. With the touching of a key, we have available to us that which, in the past, had required us to open and read many books. More and more we have less to do as computers take over much of our thinking, looming ever larger in every area of our lives. Not only do computers play a large role in the workplace, in schools and in our homes, but they have gained a stronghold in the arts as well.

We have long been aware of problems posed by the growing disparity between progress in science and the aesthetics of man. We are aware of the dangers this poses for the whole world. The danger exists as well for the quality of the life of the individual. The benefits of science come with strings attached. As wonderfully capable as these machines are, they cannot measure up to the capabilities of the minds which they appear to emulate. They cannot have our imagination and intuition. We really need not fear that computers will take over our thinking for us, unless we give in to a preoccupation with their achievements to such an extent that we no longer seek to stay in touch with our intuitive source. The mind may not serve up answers as economically as the computer but this is far outweighed by the mind's ability to reach into vaster areas. It is as though it were endowed with its own radar beams to help scan the inner space, and thereby enabling us to enjoy the almost imperceptible unfolding of each of the layers of consciousness surrounding the interior of our minds. In the mind, the same elements to which everyone else has been exposed will combine and emerge in ways that are unique to each individual. Each of us is given the gift for integrating impressions, both intellectual and emotional, and for expressing these in ways that are not only different from those of others but are ever changing for ourselves.

We could easily be pacified by all the toys available for grown-ups, some that ease our work and others that focus our attention on looking and feeling good. There is much pressure from a media full of oversell; and where there is money to be made, the sell will be expert and the come-on strong, fortified by psychological perceptions long studied and developed for this very purpose. There is seemingly no limit to what these machines will be able to do for us, if we let them. Just as there are machines now that practically do our physical exercise for us, there may soon be some invention that helps us zoom into our intuitive-creative center. We need to be on guard against unwittingly being deprived of experiencing our own existence, and not be willingly manipulated to the contrary. Eliot Hutchinson, in his book *How to Think Creatively*, spoke of the importance of individual creativity in our time. He described people who are able to retain their creativity, "who find in creative life a zest and fulfillment that makes ordinary existence pointless by comparison. Creation is a way of life much as it is an act of production and in it men find an antidote to that flat uniformity and spiceless mediocrity which too close contact with the present gadgeteering world tends to produce. And in it, though in small degree, many find salvation from boredom, rescue from standardized amusement, and a sense of fulfillment of individual destiny."

The more technical our world becomes, the more essential it is that we see the whole of life as an art form, protecting the creative nature of mankind from an exclusively symbiotic existence with electronics. We need to protect nature's provision for the individual's right to fulfill his own spiritual growth along with his physical development. With the passing of time there may be fewer areas for the rugged individualist to explore. Although vast celestial space is such an area for many, on earth our wilderness areas are becoming ever fewer. The areas in the working world in which one can carve a unique niche and apply their training and capabilities in their own chosen way is also shrinking. The situation is much different with one's inner space. No sooner is it explored than it wants to yield up new territories potent with new discoveries resulting in ever changing ways of viewing life around us. We find ourselves relating differently to all we know as a result of these journeys within.

It is within this climate of kaleidoscopic, fluctuating perspective that renewal becomes possible. All creative expressions, whether they relate to ordinary activities or whether they are in themselves works of art, are extensions of an inner experience and bring a quality to our lives that is independent of the structured influences of society. The buoyant force that is the energy of creative effort may be the one thing that will preserve individuality in an increasingly highly prescribed society with its noise of machinery and piped music, its crowded living conditions, and standardized amusements.

But the future looks optimistic, because there are perceptive people who realize that freedom of creative expression should be nourished throughout the educational process. In addition, there is great individuality being expressed in everything from modern styles of dress, in which all sorts of unlikely combinations are matched, to the visual arts in which anything and everything is being shown. In music, the role of improvisation in contemporary compositions is always increasing, calling on greater exploration and exploitation of the performer's creative potential. In the performance of older music, we are reaching into the past, unearthing the instruments for which the music had originally been written, researching the authentic styles of each period, and exploring the improvisatory styles of performance the music demanded and from which we have disassociated ourselves for too long.

Fortunately, the gates are opening wide again to this art and it seems inevitable that improvisation will be developed as part of everyone's musical training. Improvisation actually promises to occupy an even broader position than it did in its heyday during the Baroque period. The rediscovery of improvisation will contribute much towards the preservation of the individual in an age in which electronics reign, robots are becoming more and more like humans, and in which we wish to prevent dehumanization at all costs!

THE MIND'S INFLUENCE

THERE ARE MANY societies in today's world where art is a democratic aspect of daily life and where every person is considered an artist. This usually applies to the countries we call "third world" or "developing," because they have not advanced technologically and socially according to our standards. We tend to overlook the many beneficial aspects of their societies. They have retained certain qualities of life that are easily lost in the kind of sweeping changes that our society has experienced. The artist who is always on the lookout for ideas to stimulate new directions in his own work is more apt to recognize these qualities. The African Art Museum in Washington, D.C., has a special exhibit in which each African sculpture is displayed next to a painting by such artists as Picasso, Braque, Modigliani, Gris and others, beautifully illustrating how these sources influenced our modern artists. The African sculptures are by unnamed artists, whose identity is unimportant because a hierarchy of artists does not exist in their own countries. In our culture we have created an aristocracy within the arts, and it is important to the benefit of all society that the arts be democratized. There will always be artists whose work will stand out like Mount Olympus among countless efforts that are mainly of interest because they represent the fact that somewhere one more person was exploring his inner world and translating it into artistic expression.

Formal education has long failed to develop or even encourage creativity in the students held captive within its unimaginative control. From early childhood there has always been ready discouragement, sometimes of a threatening nature, from parents or teachers who feared deviation from the routine of standard accepted directions. In *Musical Improvisation*, Derek Bailey discusses the European musical legacy and its effect on our educational system. He describes it as "formal, precious, self-absorbed, pompous, harboring rigid conventions and carefully preserved hierarchical distinctions; obsessed with its geniuses and their timeless masterpieces, shunning the accidental and the unexpected; the world of classical music provides an unlikely setting for improvisation." Although I don't wholeheartedly agree with this description, it is true that the climate for improvising leaves much to be desired. The fact that we have our giants whose music continues to be performed and heard all over the world daily, in the practice room, at the lesson, in concert, and on radio and television does not justify belittling even the barest artistic or creative endeavor of the most humble member of society. Starting with this thought, this book is dedicated to offering to its readers encouragement and some ideas to work with in their first attempts at improvisation.

It is important to be aware that the same mind that engenders creative productivity of all kinds is capable of restricting that same productivity with thought that is not necessarily creative. When thoughts arise that criticize or even question the worth of the effort, the effect is always an inhibiting one. The inhibition can range in its influence from merely diminishing the potential quality in various degrees to being heavily destructive, enough so as to paralyze the action altogether. We generally carry a myriad of negative attitudes in our minds with regards to venturing forth in creative activity. These negative thoughts are like imprints on the mind from the past and appear at the most unwanted moments, mimicking their original source. Often when such phrases arise you can almost hear the voice of the person in your life who first uttered the words. Sometimes these words may not even have been directed at you. You might have heard someone else being described as talented with no mention of your ability and you automatically excluded yourself from that possibility. This is only one example, but it covers a broad spectrum of responses stimulated by this kind of thinking. Such responses hinder any effort, but especially the effort required in music-making, particularly when it involves creativity.

The word "talent" has probably caused more harm than most words to describe one's capabilities. It has singled out individuals to become self-conscious of their share of universal gifts and it may have even burdened them with the feeling of obligation to produce under the watchful eyes of the bestower of the title. It has certainly encouraged a feeling of separation from others based on a sense of being different, or in some instances, superior. It may have influenced some to choose a profession different than that which they might have otherwise chosen, had there not been this kind of attention from admirers and stimulation by the regard of others. In some instances where the quality of "talent" was not recognized, sensitivity to outside opinions might have discouraged further effort. Whether it starts in the family or within the educational system, the attitude behind such classification has a lasting influence on its victims from which it may take years to free themselves.

The young child displays untutored eagerness to explore and experience everything that comes his way. Sometimes from moment to moment you can observe the learning process as it is expressed. The child is wide open, unprejudiced, uninhibited, spending his responsiveness as quickly as it receives and absorbs impressions. Each adult has started out this way and with few exceptions has been drawn away from these natural conditions in the process of receiving the kind of education that is so prevalent. The system of education imposes a sort of dictatorship on the student, with its stifling ways of foisting knowledge upon children. Knowledge that is predetermined by masterminds and is doled out in a prescribed manner and tempo with little concern for the child's willing receptivity. These same impositions are not so easily tolerated by adults, although many have become conditioned to accept them. There is no need and no excuse for such rigidity in education, especially with the high degree of failure that is evident, and the lack of cultural understanding with which too many adults graduate.

Such rigidity in a musical education can be damaging. No matter how crude or unpromising, the students' early attempts at improvisation should not be discouraged. Stravinsky said, "Judge the tree by its fruits then and don't meddle with its roots." In far too many instances, the roots have been frozen so that there seems to be no possibility for any fruit to develop. But musical improvisation can provide important outlets for musical creativity and it should be reinstated in the experience of each person who learns to play an instrument.

Before beginning to improvise, we need to free ourselves of those negative attitudes that inhibit us, and try
to regain trust in our creative abilities. For, when we attempt to do anything while we are questioning our ability, we are being unfair to our own effort and every move
will be negatively influenced. The greatest potential
ability can be blocked in this way. It is very important
to be aware of this and to empty the mind of thoughts
that pressure us towards perfection and equate any
failure with humiliation. Do not allow yourself self-
admonishment of any sort or comparison with others as
to quality or quantity. Instead, think of enjoying a sense
of eavesdropping on your own musical utterances, giving
way to full freedom of expression, allowing yourself a full
view of the horizons you create. Claim a modest space
for your own musical explorations within the hallowed
region of the great music of the masters. You may find
yourself drawn even closer to their works as a result of
having tasted the experience of creating, finding a deeper
understanding of the process and its results. Do not be
deterred. Indulge your fancies to the fullest, even to the
extent of improvising on composed music. Such procedures have been used often throughout history and there
exists a large body of music literature that consists of
paraphrases and sets of variations based on the works of
other composers.

Improvisation is the free zone in music, where anything is permitted and considered acceptable. You are re-
sponsible only to yourself and to the dictates of your
taste. As long as the mind is in a neutral state, all judgement suspended, the creative impulse is under no threat
and is free to play itself out. Try to act simply as an observer of the nature within you that is generally under restrictions or limitations in most areas of your life. You

may find yourself surprised at what it will reveal, beyond anything you may have dared to hope for. Allow enough time to pass performing this activity so as to become disarmed and free of self-consciousness. Tape your improvisations one after another, regardless of whether you do five minutes one day and a half an hour the next. By the time you have filled a cassette there will be enough material for you to get a fair representation of your present abilities. On the basis of the various types of expression stemming from your different states of mind and mood, even a limited amount of practice will give you a glimpse of a sound palette that you would never have known was yours to use. A writer often uses journal writing to unblock creativity and to help work out problems in life, articulating things that are in his mind that might not have otherwise surfaced. In the same way, keeping tapes of your improvisations can serve as a musical journal, helping you to unblock while at the same time increasing your ability to use your natural gifts.

Expression in every art form comes in a state of release. Whether it be writing, acting, sculpting, painting, dancing or music, the expression is always released in a flow of movement. While improvising at the piano, the movements that are required are the same movements that will help free your mind of any blocking. Initiating motion frees any fixation in the mind, and the sounds that result will further dispel its hold. Our hands and arms need to be able to move freely, to carry out the impulse in groups that are cohesively expressive, punctuated where desired by sustained sound or silence, no different than in phrases expressed in speech or song. The hands must be in a free state to obey the rhythmic impulses as well as the changes in positions required by different registers on the instruments. With such freedom of movement, your music is bound to have some beautiful moments, and even if they occur accidentally (which they probably will at first), they will nevertheless be beautiful. It is helpful to know that if you have done something beautifully even one time, you will be able to do so again eventually. If you give yourself continued opportunities it will happen with more frequency, for even though you are not repeating the same thing over and over as in the study of a composed piece, you are still practicing the art as a whole. You will get better at feeding into your fingers the constantly changing combinations of patterns and motives stored in your imagination. There are relatively few basic designs that go into forming possibilities that are literally unlimited in number. Once started, improvisation is like a kaleidoscope where the slightest move effects a change in the relationship of all its parts, creating completely new designs. It is from relatively few basic designs that the greatest masterpieces have been created. Analyzing a composed work, one can identify these elements, even though while hearing the work, the general impression may be that the components were heaven sent and not available for ordinary use. Yet even the most complicated works of man have simple principles at their roots, and the imagination, mysteriously drawing on our acquired skills, is able to magically link them together.

Too often the great composers cast a shadow on our efforts, although we may hold them in the highest regard and could not imagine a world deprived of them. Many people walk through life in this shadow and are inhibited from their own modest productivity. One could visualize sitting down to compose with Bach at one shoulder and Beethoven at the other. The same block can be created when it comes to improvising. Would it help to know that Bach claimed that anyone could do what he had done if they were willing to work as hard? Would it reduce your reluctance to improvise for fear of not being successful, if you learned of at least one instance where even Beethoven had a fruitless session, described as full of false starts and disjointed key relationships? Even those upon whom we have bestowed the title of genius have occasionally had their very ordinary moments. At the same time, the very "ordinary" person may have his moments of genius. In his *Questions About Music*, Roger Sessions discusses the composer and the moments of inspiration and enlightenment that may follow in the wake of the most ordinary. Simply as a result of the laws of change, breakthroughs can be expected by anyone who applies himself to a task, even when the task involves artistic creativity. Knowing this, one should not feel total discouragement when the effort does not bring the desired results. One learns to wait out the moment, sometimes interrupting the work to return to it at a later time. Mediocrity is not necessarily a permanent state, and with a healthy objective and observant approach, one can learn from average efforts so that they can serve as stepping stones to higher levels of quality. In *Themes and Conclusions*, Stravinsky wrote, "I learned more through my mistakes and pursuits of false assumptions than from my exposure to founts of wisdom and knowledge." One must allow oneself permission to make mistakes, errors, failures and blunders, all essential features of the landscape of learning and progress. Many great inventions have been the result of something gone wrong in the process of carrying out an idea. If the child were not allowed to blunder, it could not continue to develop and learn in a healthy way. When first learning to do something new we need to be allowed this same permissiveness. When things may seem to be going badly, there may be an integration taking place below the conscious level. When it comes to improvising we are dealing with the unpredictable and should enjoy the adventure of experiencing the element of continual surprise.

IF YOU HAVE
NEVER
IMPROVISED

THE ONLY THING that stands in the way of improvising is a reluctance to take the first steps. Without thinking about it, you have improvised in just about every area of your life. All of our actions contain at least some improvisation. Just as in verbal expression the words seem to come together of their own bidding without forethought, the thoughts seeming to articulate themselves, in musical expression too, the fingers can create orders of tones that we did not anticipate. Our tonal system and its arrangement on the piano has more possible combinations that will please us than won't, so our chances for success are built in to some degree. Trusting this fact, allow yourself to venture into the creative area of playing. You will discover abilities you were not aware you had and will find that as you play, ideas will seem to act as springboards for new ideas, all working in a continuum. You will get to know yourself differently and your self-perception will constantly be open to change. You will be astounded at the variety and number of ideas offered up to you by your imagination. Too often we are busy frantically seeking, driven by an insatiable

21

appetite for more and more, when we have not even begun to use that which is already stored within the mind,
ready to be activated and multiplied through creative use
as ideas branch off and merge with others in a myriad of
combinations.

The two-year-old child who goes to the piano for the
first time will begin improvising because that is the only
thing he can do. He has not yet been taught, therefore
he has no preconceived standards or expectations to inhibit his explorations. The two-year-old child at the piano acts most intuitively, his mind not distracted from
its natural ways. The older person is more involved in
mental processes since even without training through
formal lessons he will have acquired many impressions
and developed many skills. Out of these, we build our
own unique vocabularies. It is simply a matter of giving
release to a flow of intermittent combinations of consciously and unconsciously based expressions. We are all
born with the ability to improvise. We all have the innate
mental and physical ability to respond to situations in-
stantaneously. Seemingly without preplanning our
actions, we are able to adjust to the requirements for all
sorts of unexpected situations. Quick coordinated response often belies the fact that the action was not
planned or practiced.

Our minds are filled with echoes of voices that all
through our lives have denied us our natural ways. Often
we have felt guilty following these ways when they have
clashed with standardized direction. We need to let go of
that part of ourselves that is full of those echoes. We need
to learn to move through those mental censures that op-
pose creative impulses. Negative thoughts need to be
countered with no thought. We need to learn to trust an
all-knowing part of ourselves that is always ready to serve.

One of the most important things is to always try to be aware of the state of mind we are in. When the negating energy is strong, we will do well to wait for it to pass, as in time it will. No mood or mental state is permanent.

There are times when everything comes together, the conditions are just right and whatever the medium, there is a flow of creativity one can feel as though he is carried on a wave and only needs to allow himself to go with it. Then there are the times when nothing seems to go right. At these times one must decide whether to go at it again and again, or to walk away from it and ease into it a bit later, or perhaps take substantial time out. Sometimes it is difficult enough just to get started. One writer is known to have put one sheet of paper after another into the typewriter, and when he got to the "right" sheet, it seemed to break the spell and he was able to be productive. An innocent sheet of paper can strike terror into the heart of a writer or composer, paralyzing him temporarily. There is the temptation to shy away from any beginning, and often one goes from one task to another, to do anything but face the initial involvement. There are techniques for coping with such blocks. Aside from working through negative states of mind, the writer frequently practices warming up with writing that is in the character of a stream-of-consciousness flow, or free association. A word repeats itself under the pen, or follows another without any intelligently reasonable connection. It doesn't matter. The most important thing is simply to get into motion. It can involve long or short phrases. This is not the time for evaluating, but simply for getting started. The corollary at the piano could be to do a series of musical doodles. The writer can at a later time look over the words to see if there is anything salvageable, either in itself or as a base or springboard for other ideas. A cassette recorder can serve the same purpose at the piano. Know ahead of time that you may be intimidated by your awareness that the cassette recorder is "listening" to you. There is no better way to cope with this than to simply face the fact, accept it and proceed to play right through. It has been my experience that after a few moments of self-conscious discomfort I have forgotten about its existence. Chances are that you will find many moments of pleasant surprise upon listening to it at a later time and you will be grateful to yourself for not giving in to the temptation to turn it off.

To actually start your improvisation, simply let your hands get into motion, let the fingers move keys one after another, let your hands move as dancers on the keys, spending themselves in various gestures and patterns of movement at different speeds, pausing at will. Experiment with sounds, explore any possibilities that suggest themselves. Even if it takes several sessions to fill one side of a cassette, try not to listen back until you have filled one side. You may then, upon listening back, already note some progress. As you relax and move in more natural ways, getting more in tune with yourself, the fingers will catch keys in a different manner, as though with an intelligence of their own, and the sounds will begin to change. Allow the natural integration of that which is conscious and that which is intuitive, all without expectations. Take a leave of absence from your usual ways of study. This is a permissive experience and any interference with the creative awakenings must be avoided. Allow the music to reveal itself rather than be sought out. The very fact that you have allowed this to take place is of greater value than any measure of quality.

Seated at the piano, you might find yourself with an inclination for no more than one tone. Begin with that.

This begins the movement necessary from which to bring this experience to life. Playing that tone or a combination of tones, intermittently let your movements come to rest in your lap. This way the gestures will not play out more than they carry within themselves, as though spoken in one breath. There is a certain sincerity of expression about relaxed movement in which nothing is forced. Start a new surge of activity when you feel the need. Allow a curvilinearity to the movement, extend it to its full range. Do this sometimes in silence, allowing it to be a silent expression of your mood, free even of the need to play itself out on the instrument. Instead of playing, perhaps choose some movements that might accompany the emotion or impulse you are feeling. From this, move once again into the playing, the fingers playing off the gestures. You may play a phrase this way and pause. Such pauses are as important as the sounds—in some ways even more so. Think of the dancer who has moved through various steps and come to a stop, poised in a position. Isn't that pause as valid as the movement? Playing and pausing at will, you have begun moving in your own direction and have taken the first steps in improvisation.

Think of all the ways you know yourself, all the aspects of your emotional nature of which you are aware. What moods do you recognize in yourself: pensive, humorous, questioning, loving, angry, prayerful, compassionate. Think of how you express these inner states as you speak. You are not likely to clench your fist when speaking of love whereas this action would be appropriate in connection with words of anger or anguish. Likewise a flowing movement of your hands would not accompany a state of tension. Scan your inner self for this information and try to tap into these various states of mood. Extend the mood into movement and begin to play. As our thoughts change, so do our moods, and so does the expression of the sounds we produce. If your hands playfully bounce along the keys, they will create sounds quite different from those created when your hand moves in a flowing gesture, a movement that might accompany a dreamy state. You may start with the movements directly expressing an immediate mood and as you respond to the sounds you may find your mood influenced by those sounds. This will change your disposition which will in turn change the course of the music that follows. Do not worry that this will lead to formless and meaningless phrases, because even without logical planning, you will find that some form or order has evolved regardless of the lack of a conscious plan. Some of the expressions will not be significant in themselves, but in joining with others will gain in depth and meaning. The mere movement of these ideas can pry loose other masses composed of wisps of the imagination, and more ideas will reveal themselves, some of which may have been dormant for years. Consider a stream flowing its course, creating its way, carrying flotsam and randomly depositing it along its banks, letting debris become wedged between rocks, perhaps providing a crossover as it builds on itself or simply providing a platform for more deposits; deposits that dam up the space, finally giving way to little waterfalls until one day, the seed of a tree establishes itself upon a rock that lies in the pool formed among the surrounding detritus and finally begins to foist its growth upon the scenery.

The beginning may seem difficult, the act of taking that very first step. But once you give yourself the necessary permission to start to move, to go into action, ideas and movement become concurrent. The mind will continue to reveal amazing examples of the vast richness that lies within, richness that could remain hidden in its recesses for a lifetime if not called into use. The mind is like an underground cavern submerged in total darkness, its processes revealed only when a light is shown on places formerly unseen, revealing beautiful stalagmites and stalactites. Nature sculpts herself with whatever sub- stances are available, even she not knowing from one moment to the next whether to indent, angle or curve, or whether to limit the size of one area or to extend it elsewhere. All the while, this subterranean Michelangelo works away totally unconcerned as to how this will be viewed or if it will ever be seen by others. We have no way of being aware of all that our minds have collected and stored, shuffled and reshuffled. The mind is more beautifully capable than any computer, seemingly con- taining the input of the universe. Its reaches extend for- ward and backward in time and imaginatively link bits and pieces together that we might not have thought compatible.

Why then should creative use of the mind be denied the musician? In other arts, improvisation and spontane- ous creation is a basic part of the standard curriculum. The student of painting is not likely to be told that the only subject he can paint is a model, or that he can only copy masterpieces. The painter as well as the sculptor is given adequate opportunity to create freely. The art of improvisation is essential to the actor's training and even the rigorous discipline of dance allows opportunity for improvising. In music, every half-inch of the page has to be inspected and interpreted with the utmost care to the very last dot, after which the player must dig yet deeper to discover the true intent of the composer and the ap- propriate style of performance for a piece of its time. From the start, we are asked to conform to predigested thinking, playing without experiencing the layered unfolding and discovery that so vitalizes learning. Yet some of the greatest artists have described what took place after they had stopped studying and were left free to explore, in some ways "forgetting everything they had learned." All their acquired learning was synthesized and regrouped so that it almost seemed to them that they had really forgotten all they knew. Certainly, anyone who has so seriously devoted his efforts to the study of music deserves to explore his own musical inclinations. Without restraints, allow yourself the pleasure of this musical self-discovery.

SELF-TEACHING

IMPROVISATION MAY WELL be considered a self-taught process even as we bring to it all our acquired learning and skills. The part of learning that takes place between teacher and student in any area of knowledge is, in the final analysis, self-taught. There are times when you may experience this as sudden enlightenment, but that instant is the culmination of the process of familiarizing yourself with ideas, exploring their use and reworking them to a point where an idea seems to have become your own creation, so well have you absorbed it all. With mastery over material, you are able to recognize, rearrange and recombine the components of the material in limitless ways, and your understanding frees the mind for the imagination to take over.

Many improvisors feel that one cannot teach this art to another without sacrificing the elements of the unknown and unplanned. Today, many improvisors in both jazz and classical music have practiced patterns that they have picked out of existing music or other improvisations that they have heard. These patterns have been so well memorized that they are available in a split second.

Highly skilled players are able to retrieve the smallest fragments of patterns and, again with split second timing, combine them and recombine the new combinations in part or whole with amazing continuity. The experienced listener, even when well educated, frequently cannot follow the fast intuitive thinking that goes on. One often marvels at the results which sometimes seem like a juggling act in which multiple items are going every which way. A tune is tossed up in the air and comes back down in another form entirely. It will indeed be a long day and night before a computer is invented that can even slightly resemble the creative mind's activity.

Improvisation is not exclusive to a particular stage of development or age group. The skill can be learned by the youngest child or the oldest adult. With experience and time each person becomes a better self-teacher. The very act of improvising is deeply involving, and with the playback of recorded improvisations, the player will listen attentively and with special interest since the music is his own brain child. He will learn to be analytical as he latches on to those elements in the music that please him. In making these elements part of his musical vocabulary, he will develop unique ways of organizing and classifying material in his mind so that he can return to these patterns in the future. As the patterns become impressed in his memory, his conscious thought will relax and much of the material will become intuitive and automatic, readily available for recall.

Encouraging the student to teach himself will promote successful learning. However, self-instruction is not intended to deny the role of the teacher in any way, for even though self-learning has carried some to the highest state of the art, as history has shown, this is not generally the case. Even in these rare cases, many self-taught artists seek every opportunity to study with a teacher who is able to help them achieve greater heights. In classical music, the nature of its complexities is such that everyone who is serious about wanting to do more than just struggle along has need of professional guidance.

The jazz musician throughout the development of the art has been largely self-taught, and individuality of style has always been a high priority. People like Billie Holiday never took a formal lesson in their life, yet they learned from others. Each one had an idol whom they emulated and imitated, the imitation lasting only long enough to serve as a source of learning and a filter for their own ideas. After integrating their style with another's, eventually a unique style would emerge in which traces of someone's influence might remain, but would not dominate the work enough to rob it of originality. These people taught themselves their art and worked at their music just as hard as if they had studied with a teacher.

Self-teaching does not stop even when one is studying formally, for anything that the teacher has to say or show is often so complex that the student must still go through the process of interpreting the information and examples on his own. It is the student's task to analyze the substance for the purpose of digesting and understanding so that he may function independently of the teacher. In this way the knowledge becomes his own.

In the creative arts, the greatest source of learning rests in our emotions which are spurred into motion in order to be expressed. All the skills developed for this purpose become subservient to the emotions which are the basic source of the movements involved in our playing, especially in improvising. Here you do not need to consider the expressive requirements of the composition or of anyone other than yourself. Since playing deals with everything internal, there is no one else that is prepared to tune into this source better than you. The person who might act in the role of your teacher in the formal sense can only offer suggestions or ideas which you may choose to use in the same way that you might respond to any other source of inspiration. The privilege of selectivity is yours alone and has the effect of influencing individualized ways of moving at the instrument which in turn helps to keep the creative channels open. A good exercise to explore this concept is as follows:

Seated at the piano, tune into your mood and "speak" it in motion alone, moving your arms and hands in any convolution of dance-like gestures you feel. Follow this by playing out an improvised phrase of the same general length, feeling the playing to be embodied in the gesture that preceded it. Continue in this manner, alternating the dance gesture with the playing. The fluctuation of feelings flows through this alternating activity and allows for a deep involvement and a sense of truth between what you feel and what you play. You may be surprised at some of the beautiful results attained through this inner direction, a direction which is thoroughly centered within if you let it be. In doing this exercise you will discover very natural movements in playing your instrument. Each gesture will create a unique sound, each slightly different from the next, because in motion there is constant change.

Your first sounds: an invitation to enter into the mood of your playing. Each mood innervates the hands to move, drawing sounds from the instrument. The hands themselves, as though listening, are obeying commands beyond your will, encircling a motif, dancing across the keys, drawing new energy even from the air as they do so, bringing outward that inner musical stirring. At times the mind yearns to recall some special sound, and just in seeking that sound, the mind gives way to new invention.

Let this be the most permissive experience possible. You may catch yourself thinking about the merits or demerits of the music. Simply acknowledge this gently and continue playing right through those thoughts. Try allowing that which is not pleasing or acceptable to pass, and wait for something to come that you are pleased with. It can be as if there were a cerebral radar system scanning the interior of the mind, the sensation being similar to that of trying to recall something that has been forgotten. Tension at such a moment can cloud the thinking. Allow yourself to be creative rather than pressure yourself. Allow phrase after phrase to form itself, not questioning its worth, permitting yourself to enjoy that which is pleasing to your ears and feels good in the playing. Consider anything else to be a passing thought and only capture that which allows itself to be caught as if with a gossamer net. This way one experience effects another and one phrase answers another, while gradually the horizons of improvisation expand and deepen. Harry Sternberg, a painter of some renown, once told his class that if one painting in ten were to turn out well, that was a good score. He went on to say that one should paint with the awareness that he may need to throw away the finished painting. Not a pleasing idea, but a freeing one. Always remember that there can be "gold streaks" for every one who tries, from the untrained three-year-old to the oldest person who gives himself permission to create.

With just a few tones, you can allow your hands to

teach each other. Play out any three-note group with one hand and without any hesitation imitate this group exactly with the other hand. One hand will always be releasing a flowing movement, getting out of the way of the other hand in a steady stream of flowing motion. You might come up with something like the following:

Then increase the pattern to four notes, either repeating it exactly or varying it:

As you get more comfortable, try spinning out groups of various lengths, gradually weaving longer phrases. Soon you may be able to free yourself of the exact imitation and allow one hand to play longer segments than the other. In beginning in this way with the shortest, most insignificant fragment, you will eventually find yourself playing beautiful phrases.

This approach to music is accessible to everyone. It depends primarily on an interest and desire to explore your creativity. The adventurous spirit may be frugal with ideas in the same way that someone with experience in repairing and building might pick up a piece of wire or a bolt on the road knowing its value and potential use. The process of composition goes "step by step, link by link," as Stravinsky put it. The greatest masterpieces of music are frequently developed out of thematic material that is so modest that many of us would have discarded it. Nothing is too lowly if captured by inspiration and used with inventiveness.

The cassette can be a tremendous help in self-teaching and can offer great enjoyment when you listen to the improvisations at a later time. The sounds you have made offer you a chance to become familiar with their patterns and designs, opening your ears to new sound combinations. You will retain some of these in your memory and you will find them appearing in various guises in future improvisations. Again selectivity will be working for you. Those effects that appeal to you the most will draw your attention and you will be able to repeat them. All of this comprises a beautiful and natural way of learning by your own direction.

Musicians who improvise generally agree that this is a self-taught art. As a teacher, I have learned to trust greatly in each person's innate ability to improvise. A teacher can help to open a gate and make a student aware of his own imaginative abilities. After that, the student will find his own path. There is no reason to doubt your ability to teach yourself. It requires only a little familiarity with the language of music to be able to hear the music within. There is so much to be discovered when you change your focus from looking outwards to looking inwards. Just as you can hear your own thoughts, you can hear the music that is within you.

GESTURES

IN HIS BOOK, *The Alexander Technique: The Resurrection of the Body*, Edward Maisel quotes Matthias Alexander saying, "The kinesthetic sense holds in the life of every individual the warp of the sensation fabric, the personality's dynamic index of its body." Behind this kinesthetic sense is the gesture within which the body carries the expressions of the emotional responses. Body response to thought is visible in changes of expressions in the eyes, on the facial features, in the posture and certainly in the hand movements. All these accompany speech as well as all the ordinary things we find ourselves doing. All these things are very much a part of playing an instrument.

Before the child has learned anything formally, he will make natural movements, similar to those used in any form of play, using the hand as an adaptable unit. Even at this primitive stage, the uneducated hand is capable of playing sounds that form interesting patterns with varied expressions. The child soon discovers that hopping around the keyboard on one finger produces sounds of a different nature than when that finger is set down gently.

From these beginnings the child starts to evolve vocabularies that will change as each one gives way to another in the process of continued discovery. The child soon recognizes which kinds of sounds are associated with which movements and will remember and repeat them.

This experience need not be different in its unfolding for the adult who is just beginning. Certain sounds are linked in the memory to the movements that initiated them. With the help of memory, those sounds that are not pleasing are not repeated, and those that are, invite repetition and perhaps an attempt at variation. The mind, free from an explicit domineering direction and free from admonition for shortcomings, can make choices simply based on the appealing quality of the sounds. Here the keys are the floor to the hands in the same way as the floor is to the feet of the dancer; the movements themselves directing and creating the musical expression.

Body language affects all our playing, whether schooled or improvisatory, being influenced by our emotions and in turn expressing these emotions. As Edward Cone stated in his book, *The Composer's Voice*, "If music is a language at all it is a language of gesture, of direct actions, of pauses, of startings and stoppings, of rises and falls, of tenseness and slackness, or accentuation. . . ." The fingers play off of the larger gestures of the arms and hands, influenced at times by the swaying of the torso which contains the overall rhythmic feeling. These are all linked in a flow, the playing catching the expression of the moment. Berlioz spoke of "the autobiographical technique," suggesting that all our gestures are autobiographical when they are free, not needing to conform to any outside requirements. The psychologist and philosopher William James has written of the "tactile imagination," saying that "every possible feeling produces movement." The sense of touch alone can set off emotional responses which in turn affect the gestures that are the movements used in playing. Each movement contains the expression of that feeling or emotion which stimulated it. One sees examples of this often enough watching people talk while their hands seem to be trying to extend or clarify the meaning of the words. Daniel Kohut speaks of this body feedback in his book, *Musical Performance*, saying, "We should avoid doing consciously what nature already does automatically." He goes on to say that in the learning process "kinesthetic sense and body balance mechanism monitor our internal environment and keep us apprised of our physical disposition in space." To improvise is natural and the movements need no conscious direction. Learning to play from music is not natural in the same way, and in the process of bringing the playing to performance level we need to go through stages that will ultimately lead us to the same natural presentation that is evident in improvised playing. Improvising itself is the best way to acquire the freedom necessary for spontaneous sound.

If the player is not free to start with, it may be very helpful to work on movement apart from the playing. Of necessity, movements always return in the direction from which they originated; downward motions return upward and side motions return from left to right and back again. These movements always contain something of a curve at the point of the change of direction. Standing in front of a mirror it may be of interest to study some movements and observe how fluid they are in and of themselves, apart from any playing.

These basic movements are involved in playing the piano. The observer might not perceive how much

movement is involved in playing and how much is unconsciously exercised by the experienced performer.
These movements are an integral part of what is seen as
grace and natural execution, allowing everything to appear effortless. Except in special cases, the wrist is not
rigid but rather gives. Josef Lhevinne referred to it as the
shock absorber. To watch him play was to witness the
greatest conceivable economy of motion, especially in his
octave passages and his thirds. He was graceful and
poised, traversing space while seeming almost motion-
less. Fluidity of motion was always inherent, and tone
quality, articulation and color of great beauty filled his
performances with breathtaking moments. One exercise
given to the Lhevinne students, was to play full chords
using the whole arm, with a follow-through without
pause. (I suggest holding the pedal through one harmony
to stay more in communication with the sounds while
moving.) The release in between each chord attack was
carried out in large scope. (I suggest that the student allow the hands to reach shoulder height or the top of the
music rack.) The idea is to achieve the greatest freedom
of movement and an unpercussive tone at full volume.

With one student who continued to have a difficult
time becoming free even in movement practiced away
from the instrument, I suggested that she draw great
oversized letters of the alphabet in the air. Being familiar
with the designs, she was at ease and the enlargement
posed no problem. The height of the letters rose two feet,
the hand moving freely from the wrist; at times higher, at
times lower than the wrist. Prior to the exercise, her wrist
was stiff during the up and down movements, let alone
in movements of a rotary nature. The familiarity with
the letters freed her and describing them in the air was a
matter of ease. The size of the letters automatically in-

volved the full use of the arm so that there was complete cooperation from the shoulder. After this, the small movements that are constantly involved in playing acquired the undulating quality required for adaptation to changing patterns.

If a singer depended on the tones being created through hand movements, these movements would obviously need to be at one with the breathing. This would synchronize the expression as well. In playing the piano, too often the movements are based primarily on the required positions set up by the music and are not made at one with the breathing. While the pianist can get away with this physically, the communicative quality of the playing will be less eloquent. In this regard, attention to the gestures out of which can be born more truly expressive music can benefit improvised as well as nonimprovised music.

When movement is restricted or awkward, the flow of energy is interrupted and cannot convey the impulse successfully to the instrument. The resulting sounds are then not true to the original intent. Any hesitation or interruption of the flow of motion will affect the sound in the same way that such hesitation would affect an athlete. It may require a different kind of awareness to become conscious of the subtleties of movements as they occur and affect the playing of the instrument. Whether the cause is physically or mentally based, improvement involves unblocking. Focus the awareness on the moment in motion, imagine moving out of range of that part of the mind that is charged with negative thoughts, self-doubt and criticism, almost before acting. Moving freely with your own timing will begin to dispel the blocking.

When we play from a score, the mind informs the hand

of the directions to follow in order to share that experience, invited to do so by the printed page. The caring hand simply lifts these off the page and moves them to the instrument, hopefully to move the listener as it realizes the music through its gestures. When you improvise, there is no middle source, and your own music is given sound through direct communication to the instrument, conveyed by the same caring hand. Now the gestures are of your own invention, subservient to none but yourself, directly influenced by your mood and set to work in that same instant. It is as though the whole creative force, with all the input, resides as knowledge in the hands, and the hands can think on their own faster than the mind which relays its messages to the fingers.

A good way to experience your natural gestures in response to music is to use conducting motions. Using a recording or a radio program, conduct the music you hear. If the music is unfamiliar, modify your role to that of someone following the music, still using the same kind of gestures in a choreographed manner. From this you can simulate an improvisation. This can take the form of choreographing a ballet in which you are dancing the role of a person improvising on the piano. All the feelings you might have, including feelings of inhibition may be danced out using motions that have the grace and communicativeness of actual ballet. This can be done at the piano where at some point the movement may develop into actual playing through the impulse of the ballet gestures. It will be of interest to record this session so that later you can hear how this way of moving affected your improvising. This imaginary form of improvising, which in itself is stimulating to the imagination, in turn stimulates internalized listening to the extent that your mind is able to form the sounds from its vast store of au-

ral impressions. The mind can sort out, combine and recombine bits and pieces of various impressions to form
new design patterns and expressions. It can be like tap-
ping the outside of a paperweight that contains a snow-
storm, the least stirring of its dust setting the snow into
motion. So it is with the contents of the mind, where, as
some material becomes animated, it seems to lift and allow other particles to stir and join the activity.

Seated at the piano, begin to move, allowing the movements to take themselves from the lap to the keyboard,
keeping in motion at all times. The body and the mind
do not act as separate entities; easy flowing movements
allow ideas to be readily expressed. With loose wrists, allow the curving lines of your whole arm to suggest a
shape for the patterns you play. Let your movements be
as large as is comfortable, being aware of the space in
which you move. Play an improvised phrase using the
gesture to carry the arm through the playing, with the
fingers playing off the gesture. Each time you move, follow this movement with playing. As you play, try to retain the free floating feeling. Do not allow the fingers to
bog down along the way and interrupt the flow. Naturally, these undulating motions will undergo changes as
you accommodate them to the actual playing. Allow
yourself the same freedom of movement as the dancer,
freeing the impulses, releasing them in sounds, bringing
out heartfelt utterances. Move in flights of fancy, rearranging the sounds, extending their lengths, building
on their designs. Composing music in motion opens up
channels for ideas to move through unrestricted, the
movement itself displacing or dispersing the immobility
which is the manifestation of the block.

These could be thought of as musical doodles. You will
find that these doodles can produce no end of musical

ideas, as innocent as they are. (Playing back the tape of these experiments will illustrate this point.) Peter Yates has described the process as being similar to finger painting. As naive as this may appear, it should not be looked down upon. Patterns will emerge that no amount of furrowed brow and concentrated thinking might have yielded. As "primitive" an approach as this may seem it deserves a place in the overall scheme of loosening up with full participation of the intuitive side of the player.

When heard back, these ramblings at the piano may contain some surprises. For many adults who cannot move with freedom in improvising, relying on their minds without trusting them, this exercise has proved to be very worthwhile. Recall the writer's way of emitting ideas willy-nilly, seemingly allowing the pen or the hand itself to be in charge. Its equivalent at the piano is not found among the traditions of harmony or technical regimens but out in the open field of playing.

There are always those times when we are so thoroughly displeased with the sounds of our playing that it is uncomfortable to continue. At this point, simply invite your hands to move off of the keyboard. When you interrupt your playing, you do not want your feelings of rejection to settle into your hands. In leaving the keys, try to be gracious, much like inviting an undesirable guest to leave without hurting his feelings. It is important to keep all negativity out so as not to cut off the creative flow. Interjection of negative thought stops the flow. Gracious rejection of your modest results will not turn off the creative mind, allowing those moments to be absorbed in the overall experience. And so the hand can go on stealing from the mind's vast riches. . . .

OUT OF SILENCE

THE TEACHER OF Sumei painting tells his student to meditate with each stroke. Silence is to sound what the blank canvas is to the painter, and more. It is when the mind is quieted down from all the inner voices that a new thought is born. The moment of inactivity is a necessary part of the ongoing creative process that allows the mind to renew itself. Pauses are necessary in expression of any form so that we don't encounter an overcrowding of ideas. They help us stay centered, allowing time for contemplation. In Nat Hentoff's book, *Jazz Is,* he describes how John Coltrane sometimes practices silently, just running his fingers over the keys of his saxophone in a meditative state, hearing the music within.

Try simulating a session of improvising, tuning in to your musical thoughts until you begin to hear the sounds in your mind. (Ives spoke about improvising while shaving.) Without translating this into actual sound, let your hands begin to move as though playing, but above the keyboard. Allow yourself the utmost freedom to move in accordance with the stimulus of the idea, becoming immersed in the idea itself. Play only if you feel compelled. It is good to have the recording equipment turned on even through the silent portion so that you needn't interrupt your mental state to turn it on. You will have the opportunity to notice the effect of the imaginary on the actual playing of your improvisation.

If you have difficulty at first with the inner hearing, listen for subtle mental images such as rhythmic patterns, or the sense of a rise or fall of pitch. Try to direct these images as though with a "sound pencil," magically drawing sounds on the subconscious. You may find that you are beginning to awaken a pitch consciousness, gradually developing this as you continue. This sense relies on the memory of sound, not too far removed from the memory of the sound of speech. (We all know the sound that words form in the shadows of the mind.) Your memory bank of sound patterns will be activated and now, when the actual playing is not demanded, you will give yourself a chance to improve your ability to recall.

If you feel that you are not satisfied, create more space for yourself, distancing yourself by thinking that you are leading another person in this, conducting him in his improvisation. You could apply this to other instruments or even go so far as to imagine you are leading an orchestra with its various timbres. Or you could dance around the room and discover for yourself how the whole body's action affects the responses. Intermittently you may hum or sing to activate the inner recall.

You do not need to translate this into actual playing immediately. Do so only when you feel the urge. Total permissiveness is best and the benefits from this practice will reveal themselves at a later time even when you might be improvising in a more structured context. The permissive approach helps to loosen the tight hold of customary discipline and its attendant constraints. Remind yourself that this is your own musical sphere where you are in full charge and are free to experiment in any manner that your imagination suggests. This will enable you to discover your own styles of expression as you get more in touch with your own musical sensibilities.

Improvising can be a path to one's inner self, discovering your share of mankind's innate gifts. As you follow this path, you may encounter all sorts of substitutes for the dragons, demons, bottomless pits and trials by fire that the heroes of mythology encountered, needing at times magical incantations to get past those deterrents on the way to sought-after prizes. The mind's space can harbor equivalent deterrents on the way to the moment of truth out of which is born meaningful art. Taking on the form of negative thought, these adversaries have the power of instantly rendering useless the greatest of gifts. In an article about Zen Archery, Sonia Katchian speaks of "a thousand and one ways the archer can lose his or her spirit between lifting the bow and releasing the arrow."* She speaks of the steps taken in training that revolve around this major consideration, even after some technical mastery has been attained. She explains the importance of "retaining a good spirit while shooting the arrow. . . . The Zen archer meditates while drawing the bow." In a meditative state the spirit is immune from distraction and is involved only with the present. In his book, *Creative Vision*, Richard Guggenheimer describes the pregnant now, "where nothing lasts longer than it takes to realize that it is already past." There is something about silence that helps to draw one into the "now." In music there is silence and there is sound, there is

---

*Sonia Katchian, "Zen Archery: The Impossibly Simple Art," *Asia*, May/June 1983, pp. 34-37.

movement and there is repose. One defines the other. The repose can be either in a long sustained note or in silence. It is as important in performing as it is in improvising to experience this instant within the stream of activity. Listening, focusing on the dying away of a tone or on silence, helps develop the kind of attentive listening we need in order to enhance our ability to really hear the music, without which our attention slips away as though at recess. In all playing, not only in improvising, the skilled hand can often go on automatic, and even the impulse of energy as it moves from one expression to another can be artificially renewed. This way of playing cannot carry expression to its greatest depth. We need to learn to recognize when the fingers keep playing even though the spirit has run out of steam, and we need to learn to recognize when we need to pause a moment and reenergize. Then, the hand will be charged with fresh momentum through the movement of release and renewal, not the continuation of what was left over from another expression. This lessens the danger of weakening response and interest as an idea wears down. The mind allowed to rest and renew itself, still remains in touch with what has just been played. In improvisation, this allows the split second needed to choose whether to repeat, vary, or completely contrast the previous phrase with what follows.

All of this involves quick interaction of responses, in which the idea is carried out by the hand and corrected and guided onward by the ear. In music education, too often ear training is not carried on to a point that helps the student learn to internalize the hearing of music in the mind's ear. Some think this is a special gift. This ability enables one to improvise or compose away from the instrument. Beethoven wrote some of his most complex masterpieces after he had lost his hearing. Before him, Bach, who had no difficulty in hearing, simply disdained composing at the instrument.

Every skill contributes to our being able to channel expression into music. We may not be able to analyze the process but we can be sure that ultimately everything happening is subservient to the skill of listening. The ability to hear inwardly is deeply involved with playing, anticipating the sound so quickly as to seem synchronized and enabling us to guide it out of troublesome combinations. When we can do this, we no longer need to stop the music when we do not like the sound, but are able to choose something that rescues it and even at times creates a more interesting result. If you play a key that sounds wrong you might try treating it as an appoggiatura or a slide note, moving on to the adjacent key smoothly so that it becomes absorbed in the continuing phrase. Or you might choose to treat it more deliberately, going away from it and returning, thus emphasizing it, changing the mood of the moment with this digression. In improvising, do not allow any sound to stop you, and try not to throw anything away. It is excellent experience to learn to make anything usable and workable. In listening back to the recording of such a session, you may discover that the most difficult sections proved to be extraordinary moments in the piece, even though it might have felt at the time as though you were trying to throw a hot coal from one hand to the other.

The practice of inner hearing without the aid of actual sound helps to develop your musical memory, enabling you to retain an idea that appeals to you so that you can build on it through repetition and modification. In doing so, you allow yourself to follow a natural course where intuition takes over with its own wisdom that the conscious mind cannot better.

The following suggestions may serve as helpful exercises toward developing inner listening:

Read a sentence of a poem and then hear the words back in your mind. Read the sentence again, this time lingering on syllables in a way you might imagine these words could be set to music. Let the inflection rise and fall at will. Now repeat these sounds in your mind only. Try some sentences, letting the words sing themselves from the first reading, again only in your mind. Now try out on the piano what you heard mentally and see how accurately you assessed the pitches. As you practice this and become more adept, you might start to include harmonization. There is no limit to what you can teach yourself. Notice if you seem to experience greater creative freedom than when you play out your improvisations directly. Your imagination may become more flexible and the results more extensive in scope. You might extend this exercise to looking at a painting and let it suggest its musical response, from silent painting to silent music.

Whatever sounds you are able to hear, you can recreate them in your mind. The creative mind can use any resources. Notice how the branches of a tree move in the breeze. Use this to suggest changing rhythms; think these into musical phrases and phrase lengths. One composer spoke of how he impatiently drummed his fingers on a table while waiting for a telephone call. He ended up using that rhythm for a theme. It is even possible to listen to the ebb and flow of traffic and imagine those sounds transformed into the sounds of ocean waves. Let those sounds free themselves from their reality and take on the sound forms of phrases, becoming a structural base into which you can weave or upon which you can place your own improvisational sound imagery.

You may use your own breathing as a source. This might lead you to express phrases in a meditative way, based on the rhythmic patterns of your breathing, hearing the intermittent breaths as pauses or as the beginnings of phrases. You may find that just as the breathing influences the music, your musical ideas may in turn effect a change in your breathing.

After developing the ability to use the mind as an instrument by playing music internally, you may spend time fruitfully even while waiting in line at the bank or post office. Any sound or vision may serve as the source of a musical idea.

TRAINING THE EAR

WHETHER ONE IS improvising in a disciplined manner or a completely free style, the ear guides the playing. This takes place with split second timing, at a conscious as well as unconscious level. No matter how well developed, this capability can always be improved. Even the person who has perfect pitch may have trouble recognizing all the sounds in thickly textured music. Contemporary music uses such complex harmonic combinations that even the best trained composers will often compose with an instrument so that they can be sure they are writing down all the notes correctly. For the inexperienced player with an untrained ear, even the most simple sounds may prove an insurmountable challenge.

Learning to play by ear should be a part of every musician's development. Playing by ear has been looked down upon for too long by too many teachers, yet it is the most natural way of learning to produce music. The impressions are already in your mind; your teacher. At the same time, you are able to proceed at your own pace, with no metronome marks or bar lines dictating at which instant you must supply the correct answers. With a little persistence, playing by ear can be developed to a usable degree in a relatively short time. It is easy to feel comfortable about changing around the music you play by ear, so this skill becomes a very natural channel leading to improvising. When you have become very familiar with a song you have learned by ear, it can serve as a base for swinging out into wider paths of inventiveness. Ultimately, that song can become the environment for your improvisation.

Many teachers have avoided teaching their students to play by ear, sometimes actively discouraging it, fearing that the student who had this ability would not develop reading proficiency. There is no basis for such a fear. When a student shows a tendency to pick up the music from the teacher's demonstrations or through other listening and obviously doesn't look at the page, this asset should be appreciated and the student should simply be given enough sight reading to bring that ability up to the same level. Playing by ear is a wonderful way to develop overall musicianship. Clara Schumann, one of the greatest pianists of the nineteenth century, was taught to only play by ear in her first year of training, along with improvising and some technical studies. It was not until her second year that she was introduced to note reading.

Bearing this fact in mind, any teacher should feel inspired to devoting a few moments of each lesson to guiding the student in ear training. If you are not working with a teacher you could do this on your own by trying to figure out the notes of simple folksong or any other type of music with which you are familiar. It is important to be familiar enough with the song you choose to work out by ear so that you can hear it in your mind. Persistence in trying to find the intervals of the song you are trying to play by ear as well as recognizing and identifying intervals and their direction out of the context of a song will train your ear well. Along with developing sight reading to the highest degree possible, my students are asked to try to work on one song each week to play by ear. If the student is very young and this is too ambitious, they may prepare only one phrase during the week. The important thing is not how much material is covered, but that this musical activity is continued throughout the student's training.

In an ear training session with a student, I will play a short group of three or four notes with the pupil looking away, and then have him find and play the same group. I will tell him only the first starting note, and from then on avoid doing so again so that he has to try to retain that information in his memory. This is an enjoyable musical game that can be played with a friend or family member. Gradually the number of tones are increased and the patterns are made more complex. An assignment I give to my young students is to try and learn to play a song during the week that they might sing at school. At the lesson we work on this song. I will sing along and when there is a mistake, I will insistently keep singing the correct tone until they match it. I may need to guide their listening by questioning them as to the direction of the melody and the interval in question. It doesn't take long for this ability to take hold.

A good deal of ear training can be accomplished even without a teacher. One way to do this is to pick a key and identify it, then close your eyes and play a group of notes. Keeping your eyes closed, try to guess what you have played. You can check your accuracy upon opening your eyes. Until some proficiency has been acquired the hand should not move across too wide a range, but stay close to the starting place so as not to create a challenge beyond your ability. (This activity presumes that the student is familiar with the keyboard by sight and sound to some degree.) At each session and at any time during the session when needed, play a key and allow yourself to look so that you are sure of one sound that you will be able to relate to others. Unless you have what has always been referred to as perfect pitch you will need the security of knowing your starting pitch, so that you can relate the following pitches to it. If you are not sure of the first sound, you cannot be sure of its relationship to the next sound.

A cassette recorder can be a very useful tool in training the ear. One practical use of the cassette is in dictation. You can record simple short groups of notes, beginning with three- to five-note groups with a space of silence in between. Play these back and try to imitate them on the piano. You can rewind and play over any group that you could not catch the first time around. Persist at this practice if only for a few minutes a day. Consistency will eventually develop your accuracy. Next, try it from the beginning again, this time away from the instrument, writing out the notes. These skills will be invaluable to you in your overall practice. If you continue your practice of improvising, eventually you may wish to write out an improvisation and this will enable you to do so.

As you listen to the tapes of your improvisations, you will notice many things that might have escaped your attention while playing. You might notice an unusual harmony that you would like to be able to use again or certain harmonic or melodic patterns that reappear often, presenting evidence of your own style. Focus on these, replaying these parts of the tape. Try to replay them on the piano. Even if you must grope along toward this objective, eventually this practice will sharpen your

ear and your tonal memory so that you can retain and repeat patterns. If some of the tones do not come through
clearly enough to replicate (this may be due to thickness
of texture, for example), try to simulate the effect. Sometimes you will find an acceptable substitute. Don't bog
down at this point. If you are writing out the music, you
will be able to return to these places and fill them in at
your leisure. Together with developing better listening,
your memory will be improved, which in turn will help
your ear since it is involved in recognizing what you hear.

TO THE TEACHER

DURING A SYMPOSIUM held at California State University, Northridge, several composers gratefully spoke of the early musical training received from teachers who had encouraged them to improvise. Some had been encouraged to improvise in the style of various composers, and others had been encouraged to base their improvisation on an inspirational composition they had just finished learning. They all agreed that improvising had contributed greatly to their development as composers.

Still, there are many teachers who feel improvisation to be nonproductive. Some have even stronger opinions, considering it a waste of time, positively discouraging the student or even ridiculing his attempts. Such attitudes are damaging to a student in a way that could last a lifetime unless that student comes in contact with a teacher who can help him to overcome these effects and restore his confidence and interest.

There are always some people who gravitate to improvisation on their own, requiring no encouragement, not listening to any discouragement. They enjoy what they do and are conscious of its validity in their musical lives. But such people are relatively rare. Much more common are those who do not trust their own efforts and discoveries. This is very often an attitude that they learned early on in their education. Americole Biasini and Lenore Pogonowski, educators and authors of MMCP *Interaction*,* recognize this problem, explaining that the child enters school with a great deal of acquired knowledge and comfortable and successful methods of learning. All too often he is made to feel that what he knows doesn't matter and his ways of learning need to be changed. The authors explain that the school says to the child, "Forget what you think you know and listen to us. There is no time for your self-proven way of learning. . . ."

Composer Ernst Krenek, speaking of musical education from the standpoint of the composer, deplores music education that denies creative participation. He writes, "Music without the creative approach embodied in the so-called theory courses is a dull trade, for the creative approach—the firsthand experience in trying to do what a composer does—can alone afford us a real understanding of the creative process. . . ." In his teaching in colleges and universities he had sought ways of teaching which would result in the students' finding their own individuality, their own kind of music. He feels that encouraging the student's individual personality, rather than suppressing it, is "one of the vital requirements and the very touchstone of any pedagogical method."** Free

---

*MMCP is an acronym for Manhattanville Music Curriculum Program. See bibliography.

**These quotes are taken from an article by John L. Stewart entitled "Ernst Krenek and Musical Education," *American Music Teacher*, February/March 1985, pp. 41-43.

improvisation allows the individual to emerge, encouraging flexible rather than restricted thinking, and allowing a firsthand understanding of music to sink in.

The teacher who has never improvised and who is interested in helping the student cultivate this ability need not feel discouraged. There is absolutely nothing wrong with taking the first steps together. You may be as surprised with your own results as with those of your student. Once you have passed the initial stage of resistance and self-consciousness and have acquired a little freedom, you will find yourself using all sorts of your learned skills and you will already be at an advantage. As you open this channel for yourself you will begin to find out how much more you know on a deeper level than you have been aware of.

Using the same basic ideas to start with, different players may produce music vastly different from one another. Each person responds differently to stimulation, rendering individual results. The degree of proficiency at the instrument along with theoretical knowledge and musicianship will also have their effect. We must begin with the assumption that the student possesses the ability to be creative. The same student would be expected to show this ability in an art class. But at the piano the teacher or parent may have made him feel that to improvise instead of practicing the lesson was to be neglectful, not realizing that there needs to be room for both. To counteract this feeling, it is important to be on guard against any negative feeling that would inhibit the student's (and your own) efforts. Often simple recognition of that negative feeling will diminish its power.

Once the student has started to improvise, the teacher's role should be encouraging yet passive, allowing the student the fullest amount of self-direction. Sometimes a young student will repeat a group of three or four tones insistently, until it tests the tolerance of the teacher. But often, if left uninterrupted, sooner or later this will spill over into other formations. Sometimes the change occurs simply through the stumbling of a finger which introduces a new sound by accident and the student uses it. Often what follows becomes more interesting. (Stravinsky spoke about how a total accident could arrest his interest and lead him in a direction he would not have otherwise taken.) The words of wisdom of a seven-year-old are well worth repeating here: "Nothing can be right and nothing can be wrong." This thought should help you through those times when a youngster offers a whole piece that is pure banging. In my own experience, I have observed that this response is often a self-conscious letting off of steam, a test, and the next piece can be surprisingly gentle, containing some beautiful effects. When the banging has lasted long enough, I might gently suggest that this is a good place to end the piece, and pause a moment before beginning another. This approach will bring rewards, for the student will not have been disheartened in any way. One instant of disapproval can have a long-lasting effect.

The child's family must be made aware of this kind of thinking so that there will not be any discouragement at home. Not all parents are inclined to be permissive here, yet their understanding and cooperation is essential. It may be necessary to explain to them the importance of allowing natural progress, and that their acceptance is of inestimable value. To do this the teacher must have a strong sense of conviction about the value of such an approach before he can convince the parents.

In the very beginning, the free unstructured approach may produce some rather chaotic results, but even at this stage there will be snatches of interesting combinations. Once the barrier has been crossed, the student's own unleashed imagination will become his best teacher. Short-lived successful parts will give way to longer stretches. The student is free here to experience a vast range of musical possibilities in design, texture, rhythms, harmonic combinations, and the inventive process which is working on the run, at times finding truly heartfelt expression. Much of this would not be experienced by him through written music for years to come, his fingers freely winding around all sorts of intricacies that might be impossible for him to learn from lesson material at this early stage. Having experienced these maneuvers and having learned to recognize and reproduce some of them will greatly facilitate his later music studies. He is increasing his musical vocabulary along with his technique in a creative way. The freely improvising student at the piano more readily develops beautiful coordination from the body to the fingers on the keys, deriving a good tone because of a natural and relaxed approach. There is no need to be concerned about lack of direction in the beginning. Order makes its way into any work of art when the person cares about what he is doing; being interested, the senses are alerted and observation works with the imagination to fulfill needs of balance and cohesiveness.

The teacher who finds it difficult to accept the raw early efforts and feels an urge to "correct" the student should try to wait. We might stop and consider whether it is more important that the child experiment only with symmetrically balanced phrases using "proper" harmony, or whether it is more important that he simply make music, breathing his emotions into existence in his own individual way. Sometimes there will be extreme changes in dynamics and timing, or perhaps a tone will be held until it has died away. Sometimes the tempi will vary from one phrase to another, and sometimes the child will enjoy an effect so much that he will repeat it over and over again, entranced. Sometimes beautiful fragments will suddenly break through, complex rhythmic patterns emerging effortlessly and with a spontaneity that you hope will be remembered when the student begins to play such patterns from a written score. Be patient, even the colt is given freedom to roam before being trained for a show. Allow the child this opportunity to find within himself that which too soon might become obliterated by expected and accepted standards. The child is originally the artist that the adult might later wish to emulate. Let him be, let him have this for his own, adding to his learning and enriching every level of his growth.

I encourage the student to use the cassette recorder each time he improvises. There may only be three minutes one day, and half an hour the next. Each of these sessions, however long or short, is added on to the previous session until a whole tape is filled. By listening to these sessions the student will observe changes and progress through the different segments. Without "correction" of any sort along the way it will be obvious that improvement has taken place even within the span of one side of a tape. Playing back tapes can serve as an educational tool for teacher and student alike. The teacher can help the student identify intervals and patterns such as scale fragments, sequences, repetition and variation of a pattern, and uses of harmony, all serving to sharpen the listening skills. In this way the ear is being trained with a special interest attendant since it is the student's very own music. The student can enjoy the fact that he is using patterns that are classified in the language of theory and that he has already used these before they were formally introduced to him. This can be extended to writing down the notes heard. Any kind of analysis that can be utilized is of value. Hearing and thinking in patterns frees the mind from entanglement among small separate sounds or notes, helping the player gain an overview of a piece. This approach, as opposed to the note-by-note approach, is of the greatest benefit in developing good sight-reading and transposing abilities. All of these aspects should be handled sensitively so that the free expression in the creative effort is not outweighed by the intellectual. Here the conscious thinking process must not dominate. Always in small doses, point out these pertinent theoretical factors, always heeding the priority of keeping the creative channels open.

The student's first tape will already have moments of interesting material and as the student hears these he will be encouraged to listen closely to his own playing. It is always interesting to listen to previous sessions, and I, too, have had much pleasure playing back the tapes of even the youngest students. I can recognize promising elements, and as the student gains experience and better understanding, he will also be able to recognize these in his own examples. To recognize potential usable material in raw examples is a valuable asset in any area of creativity. The value of delaying judgement becomes obvious—it could be like trampling on seedlings in an attempt to keep the garden free of weeds.

For the benefit of the teacher for whom the idea of improvising is new, the following suggestions and examples outline some techniques I have used in the initial stages. The examples are very simple because I use them with very young children, but this simplified approach also benefits timid students at any age. At first I may not even announce that we are going to improvise and the student is led into doing it unawares. When improvising has become an accomplished fact, I may then refer to it and suggest that we take a little time in each lesson to make up some music, being sensitive not to impose it on the student or lengthen the time given to it beyond the student's obvious point of interest.

The following is an example of what might take place in part of a first lesson with a five-year-old. I usually introduce this exercise referring to it as a game of "copy cat," saying that first I will be the leader and he will copy what I play, and then he will have his turn to be the leader and I will copy what he does. Asking only that he use the same fingers as I do and that he try to move his hands freely to and from the piano, I set an example of free and relaxed movements. I start with single tones, and almost immediately increase the number so that we are playing several tones in one gesture. Starting on different keys, changing directions and adding rhythm, it is easy to form little songs in the process.

Playing a few phrases is usually enough to assure the student that he is ready to take the lead and the roles are then reversed. The moment the student has taken the lead he has taken the first steps in improvising. It is that simple. Great distances may be covered in a matter of moments as the student becomes more at ease and starts to really enjoy this. Getting into the spirit of this play brings out inventiveness. There are many delightful surprises in store for the student as well as the teacher as we proceed to what I call musical conversation. I start, the student answers, and we continue back and forth. Again we take turns initiating these conversations. The first steps seem so simplistic yet they are most effective in starting the inexperienced. The same approach, verbalized differently, is equally applicable to the adult student.

After the student is comfortable with "copy cat," I give an example of my right hand "talking" to my left hand and the reverse. The student now improvises alone, the only instruction being that the voices must answer each other. Following this, I explain the idea of counterpoint, pointing out how both voices can speak at the same time with pleasing results, unlike when two people speak at the same time. Up to this point there have been no guidelines, leaving all the playing as free to fancy as possible. There has yet been no need to think of having to fit the melodies to a given harmony or scale system. As a result, there may have been moments of musical anarchy. I have chosen such a moment to show how one can resolve a displeasing combination.

Improvising on the black keys where nothing can sound wrong even with the damper pedal down offers a wealth of immediately gratifying experiences. Here, two initiates can make their own music together. The musical experience can extend to a social one as well when the student invites a parent or a friend to join in. Once comfortable on the black keys, the student can be encouraged to use the adjacent white keys. Successful results are easily obtained and can stimulate the student to venture into more elaborate combinations of white and black keys, opening up still more possibilities.

Once the imagination has been stimulated into creative activity and allowed expression it will not be easily suppressed. Ideas have ways of becoming springboards for other ideas. Among students that have had years of training but have never before tried to improvise, there have been spectacular results. It is almost like unlocking a dam, whereupon beautiful fragments start to emerge from under their fingers within one session and repeated breakthroughs occur. It is as if the improvisational ability were trying to catch up with the other skills.

Improvising sharpens attentiveness, since everything observed is potentially useful, and the player can discover his ability to change the shape of the material he is working with. Improvising enhances the performance of other works, so that improvising and performing serve to enrich each other. Gradually the spontaneous quality in the free play will begin to find its way into performing. Within the strictest application of the composer's directions, the style of performing can make the music sound as though it were being newly created at the moment of the performance. The teacher can enjoy the rewards of watching the same student approach his repertoire with deepened interest and understanding. This was verified for me recently by a letter I received from a pianist and teacher who had taken a lesson from me in which we explored improvisation. She wrote:

> Yesterday I was listening to a piano recital tape of twenty or so of my students. A recital that took place in my home in June. I could hear the influence of my lessons used to loosen up their playing. I have in particular some dynamic examples of two teenagers . . . who have

blossomed so much with their exploration into the improvisation world.

As the untutored child begins to play, free of direction or restriction, we may marvel at his comfort with the most sophisticated dissonances as he happily continues playing right through them. We need to look ahead to the time when this young student will have reached an advanced skill level, and consider that the contest requirement for including contemporary works in his repertoire is being programmed with greater frequency.

We are in a period of conflict because there is such an extreme contrast between the music of the present and the past, and the physical preparation for the literature as well as the philosophy behind it is based on such diverse requirements. There is still great resistance to contemporary music, but no discomfort should be passed on to a student from a teacher. The student needs to be free of prejudice, and hopefully, as he develops, his ability to decide on his own repertoire will be based on cultivated sensibilities that will enable him to recognize worth on his own even when the language is strange and new.

The burden on the performer of contemporary music is considerable. Not only is he confronted with new music of innumerable styles, but new notation systems to be mastered are frequently invented to go along with these compositions. On top of this, the performers are required to do much more than simply play the music put in front of them. They may be asked to make vocal sounds while playing or to pluck the piano strings or strike them with mallets. And increasingly, they are expected to improvise. It is common these days to find works which could almost be considered a partnership between the player and the composer. At times it seems that the composer is acting as a director over the free play of the performers. One composer, when asked about the length of one of his works, answered that he did not know since he could not determine how long the performer would improvise in the given sections. More and more composers are putting decisions regarding the design and control of their works into the hands of the performers. Some leave the arrangement of sections and the determination of tempo and time value completely up to the performers. It would seem that this could lead to a time when the performer will not even need the composer and will take over both roles on a full scale. Hopefully, this role change will encourage performers to include an improvisation of their own in recitals featuring the works of others.

The necessity for exploring improvisation to prepare the performer for such changes is obvious. It will never be easy, for there are so many composers on the scene today, and each is ready to introduce a new musical speech all his own. The student's experience in creating new sounds can contribute greatly to his understanding of new music, and free improvisation will be a beneficial skill. Allowing the utmost freedom for exploring music in the creative stages can narrow the distance to understanding such music. The teacher's own attempts at improvising will enable him to be more helpful to his students as they learn such works, even if the teacher would not choose to perform that repertoire himself. The child grows up in his own contemporary period and will need the tools required by the music of his time. Having developed his own musical nature through creative participation as well as studying literature for performance will deepen his understanding and appreciation of the music of any era. For the nonprofessional musician, it may mean the difference between music being an active or a merely passive part of his life in time to come. Many adult students will drop playing altogether when the only way to use the instrument requires the time to learn pieces well enough to do them justice. Life's demands may not allow enough time for this and the student often becomes discouraged. If he knows the pleasure of improvising, he may continue to spend time with the instrument, even if only for a few occasional minutes, at least keeping his fingers nimble and his ears tuned. Even the most limited time spent in this way will inject into his life an outlet for creative expression through music. His job may be less than gratifying and there may be little to elevate his spirit, but here the spirit can soar into other realities, and he can learn to know something of the beauty of his nature and capabilities which might not be brought out in any other area of his daily life.

WORKING WITH
CHILDREN

IT HAS BEEN said that the best learning takes place
through discovery even when that consists of rediscov-
ering what one has already been taught. The young
child, unburdened with dos and don'ts, utterly free of
rules, greatly enjoys this kind of experience in which he
is free to explore and discover what he will. Every child
has a degree of innate musical feeling within him to explore. Roger Sessions describes this "primitive musical
feeling" in children, saying that it "guards against critical
and cautious attitudes that accompany sophistication."
He feels that the cerebral approach interferes with the
musical response and that the subconscious is the vitalizing source. We cannot avoid the cerebral approach in
learning, however, we can counteract an imbalance by
offering the opportunity to be creative, opening a door
to ventilate the process of intellectual assimilation at every step. Improvising allows for the interaction between
creativity and the acquisition of knowledge and development of skills.

A young child will often invent characters and stories,
playing out the parts himself, letting his imagination

create a whole world for him. The child here is creating his own form of improvisatory theater to which he brings impressions from his life experience. He already possesses the language facility with which to do this and there would be nothing strange or incoherent to the adult listening in. In musical improvisation, on the other hand, the child is discovering a new language and it will take longer for him to express himself. To an outsider, the results may seem chaotic or unintelligible, as the child explores this totally unfamiliar area. During this period, the teacher will do well to overlook the sounds that might displease him and allow the process of selectivity to take place at the child's own pace. It might be helpful to remember that critics have frequently accepted that which was previously rejected. Any rejection at this point might close off natural ways of exploring the instrument and cause the child to become self-conscious. Trust the child's ability to distinguish between the sounds, learning to be selective, dwelling on the ones that give him satisfaction and gradually increasing his span of inventiveness. It is important to remember that in total contrast to his future musical experiences where he will be placing the composer's wishes before his own, here he should be given a full lead. As the child's musical vocabulary increases, the endless supply of ideas may surprise you. As one six-year-old student explained to me, "I have all these ideas on shelves in my mind and I just let them come tumbling down!"

Some of my most rewarding experiences in working with children have come from a class of four six-year-olds. Here I allowed the young children to explore the instrument, testing its capacities and finding out for themselves what they could do with it. Often this involved the repetition of one or two sounds continuing to the point of disbelief. (I often wonder what happens to the patience a child has at this stage to go over the same ground again and again, when at a later time he may be very resistant to repeating a five-note group in practicing a part of a piece that needs extra attention!) Free to explore for themselves at full length and to their heart's content, the children discovered a myriad of sounds from which to choose. Gradually, by playing intuitively and remembering the sounds they liked, their individual personalities began to express themselves. One child with a highly developed consciousness of rhythm was capable of varied rhythmic patterns that were somewhat sophisticated and warranted the repetitious use he made of them. Another child's personality was revealed in well-balanced short motifs that seemed to match his logical, clearly thought-out spoken expression. One little girl leaned towards lilting rhythms and graceful melodic contours. Another musically expressed her willful nature with exuberant changes in mood from one phrase to another.

One of the activities the children liked most was to play "orchestra." This was a very unifying experience which encouraged attentiveness and developed the children's ability to listen to one another. Sometimes this took place overlapping two consecutive classes so that there were more players. Some sat at the piano and others played various little instruments. I had collected for this purpose an inexpensive Siamese xylophone, a German xylophone, an African thumb piano, an African lyre, a dulcimer, a triangle, a couple of small drums, castanets, an old ukelin and a few other small items. This odd assortment of instruments which I had collected over time, enriched the children's listening with an exposure to various timbres. Each child had their turn to be the conductor, and they all enjoyed exercising control; when to start or stop, when to get louder, softer, slower or faster, at their whim. The children sometimes got so caught up in this that they would sway in time to their playing. Relating on an intuitive level their harmonies would at times have extremely modern sounds.

Frequently, when the group was improvising on their chosen instruments, the players were given opportunities to take turns playing solos. Here they had a chance to practice being very alert, because no one knew ahead of time when the finger would be pointed at him and the others would be hushed, to be later called upon to rejoin the music in progress. It was very much like the attentiveness one sees exercised in an orchestra. The children enjoyed the attention given them during their special solo moments, and each one had the opportunity to change the character of the music that followed through the expression of their own personality in their solo. The children, eager and aware, were all quick to be influenced by any sounds that carried conviction.

Sometimes we would improvise as a group, three to a piano, using only the black keys with free use of the pedal. Here the sounds naturally attained a harmonic unity, and often there was a great deal of inventiveness that produced beautiful segments. The children all enjoyed hearing these sessions which were always recorded on a cassette. In duet improvisations at the piano, they would take turns answering one another as well as playing simultaneously. One child once suggested to the other, "Why don't you start something and I will pick up on it?" They took turns starting.

The improvisations in ensemble took on greater variety as the students learned to listen to one another and began to respond to each other's expressions. They might start by imitating a rhythm that stood out or by picking up on the mood of another player. At times they all seemed to have joined in spirit and their music had a sound of unity as though there had been a previous agreement as to its direction. One could sense a kind of communication that, while short-lived, made a deep impression on me regarding the potential of wordless communication.

Sometimes we would improvise using visual images to stimulate the playing. There is a book entitled *Imaginary Music* by Tom Johnson that consists of 104 pictures comprised of all kinds of notes in different arrangements and designs with musically suggestive titles. The children were enchanted with this book and we used it many times, setting it on the music rack just like an ordinary music score. They "read" the implications of the pictures and translated the designs into musical sounds. Stimulated by this, they invented their own ways of reading from pictures they would draw themselves. They would play their own pieces and they would sometimes trade off and play each other's. In this way, creative musical responses were stimulated yet not restricted.

Nature also served as a source of inspiration for the children. I have recorded the midnight song of a mockingbird perched on the top of a tree and played this to my class. They tried to imitate its songs in some of their improvisations, stimulating some real technical feats as they discovered ways of playing trills and quick flurries of sound. It was fun and stimulating for the children at the same time as it sharpened their ears and helped them to explore different techniques of playing.

Every musical experience that is interesting to the student contributes to the total development. Since interest helps to focus attention, impressions are deepened and better retained. Here they all had the opportunity of responding musically to stimuli and of sharing their discoveries with others. There were, admittedly, moments of chaos, but these always proved to be temporary. These moments allowed the children to express any capriciousness or mischief they were feeling, but I always sought to find something in the contents to discuss, making it a positive source of learning rather than one of criticism.

Over a period of time, out of the general chaotic beginnings, there emerged some ideas about the formation and shaping of phrases. Gradually, a sense of harmonic understanding began to gel as I picked up on the students' ideas, unobtrusively suggesting ways the students could apply harmony to their own creations. In this way the technical instruction that took place did not inhibit the creative momentum.

Various games were set up to teach the students their intervals, to learn to write notes, and to help develop reading by direction and pattern. In inventing these games I discovered an aid to sight-reading that served well as a melodic guide and stimulus for improvising. Placing a sheet of tracing paper over a piece of music I drew lines through the notes, discussing their directions and intervals as I did so. Then I had the student do it and we noticed the parallel and contrary motion. Skips were marked as dashes. A skip of a fourth or fifth would be more widely spaced than a skip of a third. Thus at a glance, the student could tell the difference between a phrase that moved by step and one that moved by skip. He could also identify at sight the difference between a root position triad and a first or second inversion triad. This aided sight-reading by helping the student to see patterns and become more conscious of direction. It worked especially well with very young children for whom it was difficult and tedious to read each single note. Once this transparent sheet with directional marks was removed, it served as a very general "road map" for the student to follow in an improvisation. The familiarity with the piece that was originally traced offered a sort of psychological hand-holding as the student began his freer explorations. The same diagram would inspire totally different responses if the piece on which it was based was set aside and forgotten. (This exercise also works well for adults who get just as bogged down in note-for-note reading and who welcome a guide for their early improvisations.)

With children who are beginning to learn to read music, their improvisations can become a valuable source for teaching or enhancing their technical understanding. An interesting rhythmic pattern can be taken from one of their improvisations and written out, giving the teacher the opportunity to explain notation. The fact that the study is derived from their own piece deepens their interest and enhances their understanding. I explain to them that now, with this written record, another person could play this piece. A wonderful way to solidify their understanding at this point is to have the students teach their piece to another student.

A few sessions of the children's class were devoted to making musical instruments out of found materials. What began as a playful endeavor to create instruments involving little complex effort and no cost turned out to be surprisingly rewarding. Using pieces of chopped wood and small branches, we wrapped rubber bands of various lengths and thicknesses around these, creating lyres. Each child became excitedly involved in creating a different looking instrument and listening to the various sounds they were able to produce. The sounds were quite soft, which required the children to focus their listening very acutely. Some of the sounds produced were recognizable intervals. Testing the pitches with those of the piano, we found that some formed short scales, and some even created triadic relationships. They learned how to change the pitch when they wanted to match its sound on the piano by loosening or tightening a band. We also experimented with stretching bands over plastic food containers without covers, discovering that by squeezing these we were able to change the pitches. Hammering nails into a piece of wood and moving an object across the nails provided another kind of sound.

In these sessions we created instruments upon which we then proceeded to improvise. This sort of experimentation is similar to that which Biasini and Pogonowski described in their book *MMCP Interaction*. In the children's classes they listened to sounds made by crumpled paper used in many different ways, some folded, some of different textures and sizes, contributing to the different sounds. They described many activities that afforded the children the opportunity to create varied sounds, all done in an improvisatory manner, all enriching the listening experience along with offering easy and pleasant participation for all. I too have used every opportunity to help my students expand their listening sensitivity in order to benefit their own playing as well as their playing with others. We rely upon our listening skills for everything that we do musically, both in improvising and in performing the works of others. The sensitive ear is ultimately the best teaching source we have to guide us in all of our musical endeavors, and it is one for which there is no substitute.

Through all of these musical explorations, the children in my class developed a natural coordination stemming from a flow of uninhibited, ever changing movements. Over time their finger dexterity improved as well as their hand positions. They seemed to find a natural way of playing that worked well for them. They gained a deeper understanding of the music they studied.

These children now seem to feel that the musical experience belongs to them. They have not been burdened with having to learn prescribed skills before they could be rewarded with music-making. They have learned subtle nuances in playing, their improvisations sometimes revealing beautiful ritardandos and subtle gradations of tone. They are able to play tunes by ear and to find the corresponding harmonies. They can recognize intervals and read by design as well as identify sounds that are played for them.

Of primary interest is the fact that they feel no self-consciousness about using their creativity, and by now I feel that it is unlikely that they will feel any in the future. They take it for granted, almost as though they might ask, "Doesn't everyone improvise?" It has been one of the great pleasures in all of my teaching experience to have been a part of this. Starting with timid fingers poking at keys, they have acquired a beautiful familiarity with the instrument, and I feel they will have the resources to use music in many different ways in the future, continuing to create pleasure for themselves throughout their lives. One of the students told me that he walked through his yard and recorded all the different sounds and then he went to the piano and improvised songs that the flowers sang to him. I could not have hoped for more.

Improvising, the child creates musical landscapes often far more beautiful and complex than anything he may encounter in the music he will study for some time to come, as he acquires the knowledge and skill necessary to play from the printed page. His own material provides ample opportunity to define the shapes and patterns found within it. These shapes and patterns may at times be written out while explaining the process. The child will have the incentive to learn his own music and he could be asked to copy the notes, strengthening his knowledge of them. His natural way of playing the patterns can be part of the developing of his musical facilities. This approach makes for a happy beginning and can help keep the whole experience joyful as he makes his way gradually to repertoire that will further enhance a lasting love for music. He will feel that music belongs as much to him as to all the composers whose work he will be devoting so much time and attention to in the years to come. With improvisation as a companion to his total learning experience, and by keeping it alive through all the years of study and beyond, music will be more fulfilling throughout his life.

SINGING

WHEN I WAS a child, my sister and brother and I inadvertently invented an improvisational singing game. It began when one of us complained to the other about using toys without permission. The answer was an exact imitation of the words, which soon led to the expression, "I hate you!" This too was imitated, and this time it was answered back and forth with increased intensity: "I hate you too . . . I hate you more than you hate me! . . ." This went on for a few more minutes, until at one point the mimicry took on pitches that varied, and before long we were caught up in mimicking opera. It had turned to song and it was fun enough that it became a form of musical communication which we resorted to time after time, although not always around hostile subjects!

This kind of vocal activity could take place spontaneously in any emancipated group without effort or planning, and could be a wonderfully enjoyable activity in a social get-together. Again, taping it so that it could be heard later would add to the pleasure. And what pleasure it can be, yet how much resistance there can be among adults to this sort of thing.

A few years ago, I presented a seminar on improvisation to an international group of composers. After exploring some improvisation at an instrument, the German composer Gertrude Firknees, who was one of the participants, suggested that we improvise as a group *a cappella*. Her manner was so inviting and her feelings so contagious that all of us joined in without any inhibition. Each chose a moment to make his or her entry. We were all so dependent on listening to one another in order to keep amicable pitch relationships, and not to upset the established mood that the whole experience was one of beautiful communication and became a memorable occasion. When we later listened to the tape, we found it surprisingly cohesive, and the direction of the music and the various shadings of mood were so harmoniously interwoven that we could have been performing a composed work, only perhaps with more spontaneity and involvement than if it had been written out and practiced. Hopefully you too may encounter the opportunity to experience such a musical happening. It is an experience unlike any other musical activity in which you may have participated.

We continued our improvisation now using the name of the town in Mexico where we had all congregated, Zacatecas. The natural rhythm of the name made for a jolly rendering and a lighthearted mood. This improvisation ended in laughter, not from ridicule, but from sheer delight.

Such experiments with vocal improvisation do not have to remain exclusive to a group situation. Find a poem that appeals to you and read it aloud. Notice the accentuations and the inflections of your voice. The spacing of the syllables will suggest a natural rhythmic treatment. You may move as you speak, allowing the feeling of the rhythm to extend into dance movements if you feel so inclined. This could be extended to the instrument. At the piano, speak a phrase of the poem and then allow your hands to find the melody of your speech on the keys. Allow the inflections of your voice to extend as much as possible into pitches of melodic line. Do not be discouraged if you think your sense of pitch causes you to sing out of tune. Some contemporary composers are investigating quarter tones and other microtonalities. In some instances these are used vocally while the instrumental accompaniment maintains its own tonality. This may not be your choice, of course, and if it feels out of tune to you, you may still be able to find the correct sounds on the instrument and adjust your voice to it. Don't allow concern for that to interfere with your improvising. Any time that an improvised song appeals to you, and you are able to retain it, you can write it down or tape it. All of this is to encourage you to experiment, whether you feel you can keep in tune or not, and consider it one more ability that can be developed when the need or desire is there.

In working with my students, I use holidays to encourage them to make up a poem of any sort, rhyming or not, and then have them set this to music. Using this method, the music is improvised and then written down, with an accompaniment worked out and written into the composition. For the holiday season we have a workshop program where all the music and words performed are original, based on the student's earlier improvisations. The students often present these pieces as gifts to their parents. Birthdays (or nonholidays, for that matter) can also be an opportunity for sharing one's music this way.

Throughout history composers have written and dedicated works to some friend or loved one. Without laying claim to their status, anyone can enjoy sharing their own music in this manner. Such a gift has a lasting value that can only deepen with time.

TO THE
COMPOSER

HOW MUCH EASIER it must have been in the past for the composer to find his own voice. Music heard in the home, from lullabies to folk songs, dance and church music, were not as drastically different from what was heard in the concert hall as in our age. The composer was not liable to be confronted with too many rapid changes and diverse influences. There must have been less conflict and confusion to interfere with finding direction for creative efforts.

Now, modern means of communication have exposed the developing artist to enough influences to bombard him with their number and diversity. As Guggenheimer points out in *The Creative Vision*, there is no longer the possibility for "quiet, slow and steady development of local expressions" to evolve. Now, as he explains, "flamboyant ideas can sweep across the world establishing atmospheres of aesthetic monopoly equivalent to systems of international cartel." The young composer must sift through an enormous variety of styles and influences in search of those elements that can help him find his own musical language. In doing so, he will often embrace the style of another artist temporarily, absorbing and synthesizing it, then move on to another, shedding one set of influences after another. As English composer Nicolas Maw describes it, "We can plug in anywhere we like in order to nourish our own music." As the composer explores the styles available to him, he will have to overcome the inhibiting effects of self-consciousness, to fulfill the need for his music to express his individuality and at the same time be meaningful. The greatest obstacle here may simply be the anxiety of wanting to be unique. One of the best sources for releasing the uniqueness of each individual is in improvising.

With improvisation, the player allows himself the same kind of free association of ideas that the writer uses to free his mind from the dictates of habit or from the frustrations of fruitless effort that often accompany the birth of a new work. Improvisation serves to thaw out creative abilities, freeing the composer from what Stravinsky described as the "rules by which like a penitent he is burdened." In improvisation, the composer need not worry that the results will not be unique. Here, the fingers carry out the messages of a nervous system vibrant with impulses waiting to be translated into sound. These impulses inadvertently reveal personal traits in the musical design, giving great authenticity to the expression. Through the release of natural impulses, improvisation can dredge up to the surface material that might have otherwise remained buried. Such expressions will reveal to the composer the elements of his music that are unique to himself and he can build on these examples and guide his progress.

Even when the music is not suitable for use in composition it may point in a direction worthy of investigation. At the age of five, Henry Cowell wrote out improvisations which used clusters to be played with the fist, palm or forearm, a technique he and others would continue to explore years later. Carl Ruggles explored dissonant counterpoint and unrelated rhythms in his free improvisations, elements which later found their way into his compositions. It is not easy to determine at what point improvisation becomes composition. Roger Sessions felt that the composer begins to emerge the minute he singles out a musical idea and repeats it. Arnold Schoenberg felt that improvisation and composition were even more closely linked, describing composition as "slowed down improvisation."

Whatever the starting point, and whatever the main area of interest, a willingness to venture into the uncharted musical wilderness, reaching for the interior chambers of one's mind, leads the way to discovering one's own voice. Here, as Sessions points out, although conscious and subconscious elements work together, it is the subconscious element that is the "vitalizing" one. Conscious concern with style and method at too early a stage might force the musical ideas into a preconceived pattern that is more a result of analysis and imitation than of the composer's intuition. In the formal education of the composer there is often an imbalance between the cerebral exercise and the exploration of the composer's musical nature. Development of theoretical skills often takes precedence over the development of intuitive skills and the nurturing of native musical capabilities. This happens within the rigid systems of education in even the finest music schools, where requirements often substitute for a warm invitation to learn. It should be remembered that some of the greatest composers in history grew up in a musical environment where they learned their art intuitively, only later learning the analytical aspects of music. We need to learn to trust that our ear will become more discriminating, and that acoustic ideals will form in the mind which our hands will learn to actualize. We must let the teaching follow the needs as they are revealed instead of letting the curriculum establish what we need to learn. Just as freedom of expression in speaking can open the way to greater versatility with language and concepts, so can it be with music. The importance of this freedom of expression should be considered commensurate with the discipline always considered so important a part of the musician's training.

By improvising, the composer opens up the channels of his musical stream of consciousness which can guide him in his own direction, leading him to form his own musical language. Being utterly permissive, he may open at the deepest levels those passages to the musical persona that are buried underneath all that he consciously knows. Improvising, one feels as though the music has already been in existence within and the act of improvising is simply the act of releasing it. While the same may be said of composing, improvising is the immediate articulation of that which lies within, with no race between the writing hand and creative inspiration to slow the tempo of emerging ideas. Or, as Christopher Small put it in his book, *Music, Society, Education,* "Composed music is the account of the journey of exploration . . . while improvisation is the journey itself."

The creatively active mind develops its ability to harvest new ideas from broader fields. The imagination becomes more and more agile in its ability to make alliances with new sources of inspiration for its flight. The artist may look at the shimmering leaves on a tree and allow the impression to undergo a metamorphosis resulting in a poem, a painting, a dance or a piece of music. Perhaps the eye could teach the ear to hear differently as such impressions are translated into sound. Or perhaps nothing would take place at first and the impression would get lodged in the mind, eventually to merge and interweave with other impressions, emerging much later when this moment might have been long forgotten as the source of inspiration. Why not open the channels of free association in sounds that occur when improvising and use these in forming our directions and musical language? Improvisation could reveal to the composer many new sources of inspiration. Perhaps in this way the poetry in the heart will make its way into the song of the composer.

TO THE PIANIST

IT IS POSSIBLE that we have been overlooking the best way of all to warm up at our instrument in our daily practice. There is no better way to develop a rapport with an instrument than through improvisation. Even the technical routines that may follow would benefit from starting with improvisation. By improvising, the player allows himself the privilege of waiting for a breath of inspiration, moving at will in his own rhythm, contemplating at leisure before pushing ahead. By beginning his practice this way, the pianist is experiencing the act of creating, tasting moments of inspiration similar to those experienced by the greatest composers—even if the comparison ends there.

This experience can help the performer tap into his poetic sensibility when he plays the works of others, a sensibility that often eludes the performer who is trying to fulfill the many intellectual and technical requirements of a score. It may mean the difference between an individual and out of the ordinary interpretation of a work and one which is technically admirable but bland and lacking understanding—a common complaint among critics today. The pianist who improvises may come upon solutions to the subtle problems of sustaining a singing tone or maintaining a sense of continuity through silences in a slow moving piece.

It would be of great benefit to take time from your regular practice routines, which, for many pianists, are based on starting each session with scales or Hanon or any of a multitude of similar technical exercises, most of which tend to be confining and mechanical. An artistic approach to even these routines can introduce an element of spirituality into your playing. Exploration of creative avenues will thaw out your musical spirit and tune the instrument of the self. It would be like a painter doodling in order to free his movements before beginning to work. Such departure from the usual routines is well worth the time spent, and the end results may benefit more from the creative expansion than from much of the technical exercise for which we usually find time.

If it is difficult for you to break out of these routines, you might begin by exploring creative possibilities in something as mundane and technical as one of the Hanon exercises. Why not try putting it into waltz time or adding embellishments to the basic line? Wandering off on a melodic sojourn between two notes could teach you a completely different way of exploiting the potential of these warm-ups.

Bartók's *Mikrokosmos* can prove invaluable to developing your listening and playing within a confined area, and help to free you for improvisation with both hands simultaneously. Beginning with the exercises in the first volume that concentrate on five-note patterns, allow your fingers to vary these, alternating the written patterns with improvised ones in a smooth flowing manner. You might alternate between the hands, playing an improvised pattern with one hand and the written pattern with the other. Transposing and writing out some of these exercises will help deepen your understanding of the process.

In exploring such exercises you may discover some technical routines that are better suited to you personally than the ones on which you normally rely. You may find an exercise that helps you to solve a specific technical problem you need to work out. Even if only a short time were spent this way on a daily basis, the benefits would soon become apparent. It is a sad commentary on the attitudes that pervade the serious study of music, that the pleasure involved in the process of practicing has been replaced by pressures to achieve technical prowess or meet with outside approval, goals that are irrelevant to the role music could play in a person's life.

Most of the music we study comes to us from another time and place. In order to feel the music as his own and to give a convincing performance, the serious student must somehow overcome the music's inaccessibility. Notation alone can never fully convey the composer's intent, and there is always the need to read between the bar lines. I had never fully appreciated the challenge of working through notation until I decided to try to write down an improvisation I had taped. After completing the first section, I decided to play it for myself using the manuscript. But all of a sudden the music I had found rather pleasing had lost all of its appeal. I couldn't imagine why I had ever thought it worthy of writing out. I listened to the tape again, and here I experienced the same positive response. The notation couldn't begin to capture all of the subtle effects and nuances which emerged during performance. This experience illustrated for me the role of improvisation (whether conscious or unconscious) even in the most careful interpretation of composed works. It is this essential ingredient that lends spontaneity and individuality to a performance.

In performance preparation, after all the work has been done, the ideal execution should sound spontaneous and free rather than studied. Yet there is really no place in our study that focuses on helping to achieve this quality. Totally free improvisation is the best way to foster the development of this characteristic in playing. Improvisation can be the musical means of getting to know yourself much as one might gain insight by keeping a journal of thoughts and impressions. By taping these improvisations you can keep a record of your development. You will find places in your own music that really speak to you, having come from your own heart. Even in very free improvisation you may notice that you are given to unique expressions that have special rhythmic and directional patterns. These expressions are influenced by your nervous system which has a strong effect on your responses to stimuli. The natural gestures that result in your response give an individuality to your expression and give your music a sound of its own.

Improvisation that is not tied to any specific tonal system or structural plan may be inhibiting at first. You may envision the results to be chaotic, but it is well worth braving such possibilities just to find out how much natural order there is in expressions of the unconscious mind, and to learn to what extent we can trust it. Attempts to conform to a harmonic scheme of a specific tonality restricts the creative direction and individuality. Without these conscious restraints, the player is free to explore new areas and discover relationships that would not have been accessible within a tonal framework. Likewise, any preoccupation with form or style restricts the freedom either to follow the impulse of the initial expression or to wander away from it completely. An idea may require much more space to complete its expression than might be encouraged by any given form. Allowed freedom, the expression could suggest its own formal design, giving the player full opportunity to be his own architect. The myriad of newly discovered sound patterns will suggest their own directions, and by working in this rich and fertile field of sounds, the player will develop still greater versatility.

Through free improvisation you may discover technical abilities you did not know you possessed. Patterns that otherwise might require much practice present themselves like magic. You may find yourself wondering why this hidden technical facility does not rescue you from having to diligently practice those difficult passages in your repertoire. This curiosity is felt by even the greatest performers. Jazz clarinetist Pee Wee Russell was once presented with a complex thickly notated manuscript. After protesting that he could not play it he was informed that it was simply a written out version of an improvisation he had played the night before. He still maintained that even if he could make sense of it, it would not come out the same way and it would be almost impossible to come even close to it without a great deal of practice.

Success with your improvisation will boost your confidence and lead you to find methods of practice that will allow these natural abilities to come through. Becoming aware of your technical ability in total freedom, you will not submit as readily to an overdose method of practice, but will seek out those elements on which you really need to focus. In short, you will separate your natural ability from that which still needs direction and practice.

One way to free your improvisation is to follow the example of the writer who begins by writing down his thoughts as they occur in a stream of consciousness. James Joyce's *Ulysses* offers excellent examples of stream of consciousness writing and might serve as a literary model for a musical version. Beginning with relatively few basic elements of musical speech, the mind releases material from its vast store of impressions in constantly changing combinations like a kaleidoscope, producing a seemingly endless procession of designs. With no more strategy than you might apply in natural conversation, allow your intuitive nature to awaken. Allow yourself to play any musical nonsense or inventiveness that might occur, enjoying the freedom to move at your own pace, pausing where you wish, rushing or lingering, holding back, playing now softly, now loudly, always listening, choosing to repeat over and over again any phrase you like to your heart's content. In free improvisation, give yourself all the freedoms you are normally denied.

Bringing improvisation into the realm of practice repertoire can also yield results which benefit both technique and interpretation. Working with music that is complete in itself is a good point of departure. For example, take a section of a piece, analyze the harmony and reduce it to its main chords. Play these chords in long beats, spacing them far enough apart so that you can embellish the spaces in between melodically and rhythmically. Or you might focus on a single aspect of a certain piece, a characteristic rhythmic, melodic or harmonic nuance that catches your attention. Use it as your basic motif and explore its potential.

There are specific practical benefits to using existing material. Improvising on a difficult passage frees both the mind and the technique. Extract a pattern from a technically difficult section of a piece and play with it. Play it lower, higher, releasing and relaxing the hands as you go. Both the mind and the fingers will better grasp its structure. In a slow moving section with few notes, it is sometimes difficult to maintain the sense of movement with a free flow and continuity. By transposing it and making it into a continuous chain, for example, you can free yourself and your movements without losing sight of the composer's intention.

Try imitating the style of a composer you are very familiar with. You may enjoy the feeling of retracing his path and trying to tap into his thought process. This will result in a heightened perception of that composer's music; you will take note of harmonic progressions, rhythmic patterns, melodic shapes and phrasing, dynamic color, articulation and the use of silence, things which you might have taken for granted before. In working with a piece of music in this way you may feel yourself more deeply immersed in the composer's mood and you will feel that you are beginning to understand something about the workings of his mind. To a certain extent you will share the experience that went into the creation of that work and your involvement will deepen.

Improvising variations on a familiar theme is another excellent source for stimulating and expanding your imagination. The theme gives you a secure base, freeing your mind so that it can be totally involved with inventiveness. You may be surprised at how far you will be able to extend the given theme, even to the point where the theme is overshadowed by the character of the variations. Once you have broken ground in this way, you might invent a theme of your own and use that as a base.

These suggestions are only intended to help you overcome the initial barriers that might exist for you. Use these ideas as springboards for your own and then draw from your own experience. The fact that many existing compositions were originally nothing more than written out improvisations should encourage you and help to dispel the impression that improvisation is a waste of good practice time. Through improvisation you will improve your personal relationship with your instrument and with the music you play—written or otherwise. The words of Anais Nin ring true here: "The value of personal relationship to all things is that it creates intimacy and intimacy creates understanding and understanding creates love." No aspect of music-making is more intimate than improvising.

MORE IDEAS TO EXPLORE

THE IDEAS AND suggestions in this chapter are offered as a guide to those who are hesitant to step
into the unknown territory of improvisation. The examples are intended only as general maps that may or may
not be followed and which will hopefully encourage the
player to wander off and away at will. Although many of
the suggestions are presented in a very simple way, directed towards the inexperienced player, the same suggestions may be used to great advantage by advanced
players. Suggestions that have been used successfully
with six-year-olds become totally different tools for the
imagination of an adult with much more experience and
understanding. For example, the very basic ideas suggested earlier for improvising a musical dialogue between
the hands could, in a more sophisticated context, grow
into the improvisation of a two-part invention. It has
seemed necessary to introduce the ideas in a simple manner because of the trepidation and reluctance I have seen
in so many otherwise advanced players who are beginning to improvise.

As you explore the suggestions that follow, do not

concern yourself with progress and achievement. Go as far as you like and are able to. Here you need no teacher. Trust the fact that if you keep bringing your body to the task, your improvisation will continue to grow and become more interesting.

THE BLACK KEYS AND THE PENTATONIC SCALE

Improvisation on the black keys of the piano can bring immediate gratification even to the person who has never played the piano. The black keys are arranged in a relationship that forms a pentatonic scale. When all five of these keys are played simultaneously with F# as the bottom note, these tones form a triad with an added sixth. The remaining key (G#) is the second of the chord and is absorbed in the total sound so that it does not diminish the character of the chord with the added sixth. You can play as many black keys as you can reach simultaneously, even with the help of the forearm, and the harmonic clarity will not be totally lost. Because of this clarity you may use the pedal to sustain sonorities while you give freedom to gestures in your playing, pausing as long as you like and using any rhythmic pattern to add variety.

A good exercise that will let your fingers feel at home on the black keys while at the same time limbering them into fluency is to start on F# with the thumb of the right hand and play out all the fingers on the adjacent black keys. Without pause, let the thumb move to G# as the new starting key, again playing out all the fingers. Continue this so as to allow each of the five black keys to serve as the starting tone, carrying the patterns into at least one more octave. The left hand in its turn would start with the fifth finger and follow the same pattern. Try this with both hands separately and in unison. Try it in unison two octaves apart. Within one octave, try the hands with the same pattern but now starting a sixth apart. Change the starting combinations. While the hands are in one of these positions, let the fingers play patterns either in unison or alternating between the hands to discover what combinations of sounds lie under their position. Experiment with changing the order of the notes. The first order would be 1-2-3-4-5. Other ways might be 1-5-2-3-4, 2-3-4-5-1, 3-4-5-1-2, 3-5-2-4-1, etc. Transfer the experience to the left hand. Try finding some intervals to play with the free hand as accompaniment.

A tremendous amount of learning can take place in a very creative manner as you confidently explore on the black keys knowing that you are protected from wandering into tonal problems that might be confusing. Here you can safely test out contrapuntal ideas, as there are no "unpleasant" combinations of intervals. You can have a melodic line in one hand and harmonic accompaniment in the other without jarring results. You can use clusters and glissandi. You can combine the use of the sostenuto pedal to retain one sonority while you superimpose all sorts of movements over it. This kind of warm-up exercise on the black keys will immediately open you up to many possibilities, broadening your musical vocabulary right from the start. Also, learning to play on the black keys may reduce the trepidation you feel when you see the numerous sharps or flats in the key signature of a piece. You are more likely to regard them as directing you to do something that you have already done.

Using the pentatonic scale of the black keys as a base you can form a number of interesting scales creating new tonalities by merely adding one white key to the series.

Each time you change that white key the character of the scale will change and that will change the direction of your improvisation.

It is but a half step from playing on the black keys to playing on the adjacent white keys above or below. Try a tremolo of clusters using the flat of the hand, one on the black keys, the other on the white. Experiment with this tremolo by beginning slowly and softly, gradually increasing to fast and loud, or the other way around. Next, instead of using the clusters harmonically, separate them, arpeggiating the notes and turning the clusters into a scale. Play a dialogue between the two hands, still with one hand on the black and the other on the white keys. Play the melodies in each hand simultaneously. You will be playing in a bitonal system. Experimenting with bitonality will expand your listening skills and increase your inventiveness.

IMPROVISING YOUR OWN EXERCISES

Choose any cluster of keys at random that lie completely under one hand. Turn this into a five-note scale playing one key at a time. Repeat this a few times in the same direction until you achieve a smooth cycle. Teach this to the other hand. Use the hand that is more comfortable and better coordinated as an encouraging model for the less comfortable hand. Start in a low register allowing at least four octaves and use the left hand to begin, alternating the hands, crossing them over each other to make one long ascending line. When you have mastered this, try it with one hand, listening to reproduce the same flow as when the hands alternated. This serves as an excellent example of how the ear and a sense of confidence negate any technical problems. You have heard the lines played in an unbroken stream and this becomes the image in your mind's ear, the model which you now imitate with one hand. The best way to work with this idea is to keep alternating the two ways of playing the passage so that first you hear the model and then the imitation. Keep repeating this and see if after a few times you begin to notice a closer resemblance between the example and the imitations. Be sure to allow for a release at the end of each run before starting again so that you have a new momentum. Think of doing it on the run, not stopping for any finger that might have missed its mark. The whole process can then be reversed, starting at the top and going down. You might like to exploit the cluster still further by rearranging its order or by starting on the second, third, fourth or fifth note of the pattern. With each slight change, the pattern becomes completely changed. The same cluster can be used as a basis for improvising a melody that stays primarily within its confines. Try a number of different examples to explore some of its possibilities. When you have begun to feel sated with this five-note group nucleus, add one note. This will open the way to many more possibilities. Along with feeling a sense of release from previous restrictions, you will enjoy the new melodic and harmonic stimuli. Beginning with an economy of material develops versatility.

PLAYING WITH NUMBERS

Since at least the eighteenth century, numbers have played a role in improvisation. One popular game consisted of rolling dice and using the numbers that came up to create a melody. (Mozart even claimed to have composed by rolling dice!) It is great fun to see how much one can do with melodies formed from numbers which are then converted to the degrees of the scale. With my own students, I always take advantage of telephone numbers, which offer an open-ended source of ideas. They enjoy the novelty of hearing their telephone numbers turned into musical pitches forming a melody. When it doesn't translate to a pleasant tune, we work with it, adding a note here or there until it is pleasing. Sometimes, simply by holding one note longer and contracting the time of a pair of notes that follow, it becomes acceptable without adding any new notes. Sometimes I give a student the assignment of writing out in notation his telephone number repeated on ten different staves, leaving enough room to fill in one or more notes between each of the original notes. From this we create ten different melodies from one telephone number.

The following scale chart shows how these numbers are converted to scale tones. The numbers one to eight are used within the octave. Nine would be the same as two only an octave higher. For the ten you may choose to use a rest or you could give it the power of substituting for any number (note) of your choice.

Example 3A:

The telephone number transcribed below is the one used to call for the correct time. The three melodies that follow it offer examples of how one might begin to expand on the original melody. The square-shaped notes represent those of the original melody.

Example 3B:

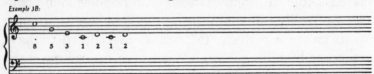

These are but three simple examples, and again, as with any kernel of a musical idea, the possibilities extend *ad infinitum*. They could be played slow or fast, loud or soft, depending on what mood or character you choose. You might try harmonizing them, using any style you like. Setting the same melody in a Debussyesque harmonization will yield an entirely different kind of music than if you were to seek the sound of Bartók, for example. Or you might try basing it on the simplest harmonies, putting some ornamentation to use. Your own telephone number could be varied in so many ways as to be hardly recognizable and could become the source of a good chunk of material used for improvising or even composing.

LENGTH OF A PHRASE

What determines the length of a musical phrase in free improvisation? Starting out, we may have no inkling of its ability to regenerate itself as it progresses. Some inner motivation stirs it into being and the phrase seems to contain its own momentum, unfolding its future through the interplay between the conscious and the intuitive mind. A flash of an idea can inspire a rash of patterns in its wake. A phrase may seem to have already spent itself when at the same instant another strand of melody emerges, the thread unbroken, its energy somehow re-generated along the way. It is as though the music were woven on a flexible loom that could expand to meet the needs for design that continue to evolve. A few tones be-gin, beguiling others to follow. Sometimes a fragment is repeated on another pitch or completely reversed like a Rorschach test. At times, each successive group suggests new directions, new patterns, all containing an element of surprise as the process unfolds, spanning time like a suspension bridge over a gorge, even carrying the lis-tener across a silence that might intersect the flow of sounds.

Try the following: Improvise a phrase of any length, holding the last tones or chord until it fades away or sug-gests a continuation linked to the fading sounds. If you feel no urge to continue, let it close at that point. Listen-ing as you hold those last tones gives your mind a chance to clear itself, allowing it to respond to any suggestion that might be revealed by any strand of the musical fab-ric that catches your attention. The best results will de-pend on your being observant and honest, knowing whether you really feel impelled to continue or whether you are trying to manipulate the length of the phrase. It is in this state of sincerity that your music will have a sound of authenticity, a quality that can tolerate any shortcomings that may exist.

From one note to another one can find enough differ-ent melodic paths to keep the imagination busy for a long time. You can start with two adjacent keys. Imagine that you are winding a garland around a pair of tones. It is an easy and pleasant way of improvising on a very small scale. At the same time, because of its restricted boundaries, it lends itself to much freedom as there is no danger of getting into too many predicaments of tonality. Gradually increasing the span in between the two tones, play an auxiliary group by going up to the next key and returning. Add one more note in between each time, as shown in the following examples. Use stepping or skipping intervals, varying the rhythms where you wish. Since you keep returning to the starting point which is easy to keep in mind as the destination, this is a good exercise for learning to extend the length of a phrase without wandering off into another tonality. In playing out such an exercise, it is best to pause an instant between each version so that the sameness of the unchanged part of the melody does not dull your listening acuity.

Example 4A:

The above example is carried out within the restriction of keeping the main part unchanged. When you are comfortable with this, try starting with a five-note group and freely choose your way in between, still using the same note as a goal, gradually adding as many notes as you wish and repeating or not repeating as you choose.

Example 4B

BEGINNING WITH TWO VOICES

Improvise a melodic line in unison between the two hands. Move to different registers from one phrase to another. Play on but now space the melodies two octaves apart. Note the change this brings about. Try single line melodies a third apart and a sixth apart. Using the interval of a fourth or fifth will give you a feeling of the old chants. Try something in seconds, then in sevenths. Try spacing the sevenths two octaves apart.

Play a single line melody against a drone bass, establishing a reference point. Move away from this bass, every once in a while returning to strike it again. This will keep you rooted while you give your melody free reign. Try the same melody in chords. Use bitonality, use any altered chords that fall under your fingers. All these experiments will show you interesting examples of how a melody can be treated harmonically.

VARIATIONS

You might try playing a set of variations on a familiar melody. The more simple and familiar it is, the more the imagination is free to participate. Variations offer a good opportunity to be inventive and to make use of all your practice and acquired skills. It can be like taking a theme on a series of adventures. If at first you feel there is not enough variety in your improvisations on the theme, you could make out a list of ideas or techniques you could use which exploit every device in your musical vocabulary.

A certain harmonic progression may hold special appeal for you. Analyze it, making up little studies using it. Practice it in different keys. Try building an improvisation around it. The simple chord progression on which Greensleeves is based might serve as an example of what you can do. The example below might help to start you off. The first variation employs a simple arpeggiation of the chords. In the second variation, the chord notes are filled in melodically, and the third variation begins to expand on the melody itself. This is good practice for becoming versatile with melody, teaching you how to expand motifs and develop ideas.

Example 5A: Theme.

Example 5B: Variation I

Example 5C: Variation II

Example 5D: Variation III

It can be great fun to improvise a group of variations, setting each one in the style of a different composer. On whatever level of understanding you relate to the music

of these composers, there will be some aspects that especially impress you. Try to identify some element of the
music that you could use as a base, some characteristic to
which you feel a particular response. People often make
notations in the margins of the pages of books they are
reading that evoke a response. It is like having a dialogue
with the author. Entire compositions have grown up out
of this sort of urge and have become homages to the
composer that inspired them, even though the new work
might be in an altogether different style. *Hommage à Ra-
meau* by Debussy is but one example.

Regardless of what style you choose as your medium
for expression, studying the variations of Mozart and
Beethoven can supply you with many excellent ideas and
stimuli for exploring the various treatments you could
apply to the simplest folktune. To study Bach from this
standpoint is to learn how many lives a short phrase may
be given.

CHANGING SHAPES OF MELODY

An inspiring theme does not always present itself. It is
good to learn how to change the shape of whatever does
come to you until it finally pleases you. Beethoven's
notebooks are full of examples of the way he worked with
themes, constantly changing them until they became acceptable to him. The example below offers a theme that
could be considered an "ugly duckling."

Example 6A:

The following two versions of the same theme show how drastically its character can be changed by filling in some of the wide melodic intervals and adding a left hand part. These versions are transcribed directly from improvisations using the original theme as a base. (The notes of the original theme are notated as squares to make it easier to see how the theme has been altered.)

More than once, Stravinsky has written how an accident or mistake has led him in new directions, enabling him to find something useful in the "commonest and humblest thing." In his book, *Poetics of Music*, he tells us, "One does not contrive an accident; one observes it to draw inspiration therefrom." While the example shown here was not based on an accident, the model contained some of the jarring effects of one. Give a second thought before discarding a seemingly unworthy idea. In trying to work with such material, you will develop agility and inventiveness. If your melody has wide, unwieldy intervals, you can fill them in with slides and runs. If the progression is stepwise but doesn't sound good to you, this may be an opportunity for you to use ornamentation to improve it. At times it only takes moving from one tone to the next to alter an unpleasing effect. This may become one of your most important skills.

If you have gone this far, you are probably finding yourself doing some fairly interesting and pleasurable improvising by now. The few suggestions here have been offered as avenues to aesthetic experiences in musical creativity which will hopefully reveal many more ideas in the process of exploring them. Everything we are working with, every musical building block has been in use for countless generations. There is really nothing new here. Yet from these building blocks each one of us can create music that is unique. The innumerable combinations of these same elements offer no end of possibilities. Once started, the mind learns how to play this game and begins to create its own challenges. Each experience can lead to beautiful music. The only requirement is that there can be no criticism or rejection that will alienate you from your musical attempts. Remember that there is always something salvageable in the least satisfying phrase if you learn what treasures can be extricated from artistic waste.

EPILOGUE

R ECENTLY I HAD the opportunity to discuss improvisation with Naima Prevots-Wallen* and Paul
Gleason,** two artists whose work and ideas about
teaching I admire greatly. Since much of the conversation strongly reinforced the ideas presented in this book,
it seemed that sharing some excerpts from the discussion
would be a fitting way to end it. The discussion was
taped and I have transcribed it exactly as it transpired,
not filling out any incomplete sentences or altering im-
perfect grammar. In this way I have tried to keep the
spontaneity and vitality of the dialogue intact, hoping
that its enthusiasm might be communicated to the
reader.

---

*Naima Prevots-Wallen's career in the arts has encompassed many en-
deavors. She has been a choreographer, performer, educator, administra-
tor, writer, scholar, critic, arts consultant, and museum director. She has
been a leader in arts education and a consultant to the National Endowment for the Arts, the National Endowment for the Humanities and
other organizations. Recently she has been developing a variety of pro-
grams for the Hollywood Bowl Museum for which she created their first

GLEASON: It has become so difficult for an aspiring artist who has worked so hard for so long to find a place where he can be joyful in sharing his developed gifts and feel like a respected citizen. It has taken all my life to realize that if you use your music in the park or in your living room just with your family, it's all right. I am able to say this to a student in whom I may recognize the potential artist. It took me all my life to be able to realize this for myself and say this to my students.

CHASE: How fortunate for your students. Too many of the greatest teachers have neglected to express this to their students, even when they have been aware of the narrow openings at the end of the long hard period of greatest effort spent in developing their abilities. So many who could not find a proper place to use their music are left with this feeling of failing their teachers, their schools, their parents, their friends. Many of these students unknowingly have been working towards a di-

---

exhibit and catalogues. She has been awarded a Senior Fulbright Lectureship to Australia to work with universities in developing curriculum and to help create dance archives. She has also received a fellowship from the National Endowment for the Humanities.

**Paul Gleason is the artistic director and producer for the American Center for Musical Theater, and is a nationally known director, producer, and teacher in musical theater and opera. He also serves as a consultant in the performing arts and was recently appointed to the New American Works Panel in the Opera-Musical Theater Program for the National Endowment for the Arts. Through his career he has appeared in a number of television shows and thirteen feature films. He is a devoted teacher of theater and was chairman of the graduate acting program at the Pasadena Playhouse. He has coached such notables as Richard Chamberlain, Mary Tyler Moore, Ann Jillian, Joanna Gleason, and William Katt. His latest assignment has been to choreograph for John Huston's new film which is based on the James Joyce novella, "The Dead."

ploma in negativity. You relieve them of this possible end result. It reminds me of a young artist who was on the faculty of a university, teaching art and continuing to paint, and yet he did not feel that he had fulfilled his mission. He said that the day he stopped thinking of himself as a professional artist (although he kept functioning in that capacity), he felt much relief. I can't help but feel even more convinced as you talk, of the need for improvisation to be given an important place in each one's musical experience. For this is truly an area that is totally independent of any outside connection, and one's living room while improvising could become The Met.

After some discussion, the conversation turned towards teaching and our theories on education. I showed an example of diagramming music from a page as an aid to reading music.

PREVOTS-WALLEN: What you are really talking about is not just technical education, you are talking about conceptual education, about really understanding music, building a base of understanding and feeling. Music does not exist in an isolated context. What you are doing is reinforcing what you are doing in music by relating it to other things and that gives the child or adult a deeper sense of the music. What you just showed us makes a lot of sense because you are integrating the sensory motor experience with the totality of learning. This is a visual thing, it is an emotional thing. It goes back to Dalcroze. This action is a movement action, and that action can aesthetically relate itself as it sends a message to the brain. That message is both a movement message and a tonal message. It's not just one message. You are finding lots of ways of reinforcing musical sensitivity but not by just emphasizing the technical. . . . What you are discussing relates to education in general and goes back to a long-standing argument regarding rote learning or conceptual learning. Jerome Brunner wrote about this in his book, *Toward a Theory of Education*. Teaching a child to read by just mastering the letters only goes so far because teaching is understanding, music is understanding. Teaching the notes, you may get very quick results but then what?

CHASE: Clara Schumann's father only taught her to play by ear, improvise, and do some technical studies until her second year. Only then did he introduce the notes.

GLEASON: I'm working with sixteen actors at the moment, none of whom are dancers, and I have to teach them choreography and teach them a Lancer's Quadrille for a new film for John Huston. He doesn't want them to look like dancers doing this dance but like ordinary people who have known this dance as they were growing up. They may not have been trained dancers but they would have been trained in this dance. So there needs to be an improvisatory feeling about the way they end up doing this. Many things contribute to this. For one thing the original authentic version would be about forty-five minutes long, and whatever country it would have been danced in, there would have been some different ways with it. Without demonstrating, and not going into the details of the steps, I just indicate that you start out by going this direction and then that. We are going at it in an improvisatory manner and allowing the big movements the use of the big muscles first. I have to think that art, by definition, is a natural thing. They are starting out doing things they would do in walking naturally and rhythmically. When they were out of time, I did not ask them to count at this point because this would make them concentrate on little muscles. I simply suggested that we try to do this together. Finally they were all doing it together. Through this they were improving their ordinary way of walking just as the arts improve the common man.

CHASE: I have visions of improvisation enriching the lives of the so-called "common man" in every walk of life, and that is why I'm so interested in knowing other ideas for integrating this among the different disciplines. In his book, *Education and Ecstasy*, George Leonard described nonverbal types of communication between people. This could be another way of investigating this, as all the senses are alert when joining in making any kind of art. In the children's class, this was evident when they were playing together and one child was leading. They managed to be quite together in their getting louder or softer, slower or faster, picking up on one another's mood. Sometimes, some of the children danced through this. It was a beautiful togetherness. An adult party could be planned to allow for a creative happening. At one party I attended, this did take place. Two people were improvising, and were having a wonderful time with it, and decided to invite everyone to join in by helping themselves to anything they could find in the kitchen, a wooden ladle and a frying pan, some glasses to be struck, an item with ridges that produced an interesting effect when an object was run against it; some nice music was made and everyone was able to enjoy taking part.

PREVOTS-WALLEN: I am thinking that people getting inside themselves and learning by doing things is what we are talking about. We are talking about the kind of learning that is scary to some people because it is not as specific to certain ways they are used to. The teacher has to have confidence to help and that confidence is in relating to students. You are relating your confidence to your students, so your students don't question it when you go off the beaten path. . . .

GLEASON: Is your book titled *Improvisation?*

CHASE: I'm considering a title like *The Motions and Emotions of Improvisation.*

GLEASON: That's interesting, because earlier, when I was describing the choreographing for the film, in discussing guiding the actors in the large motions, with the large muscles, I had wanted to add that when you quell motion, you quell emotion. When you work with larger motions with your students, you are helping them to express emotions. What happens in teaching penmanship is, "don't move your elbow, don't tilt your pen," in teaching piano, "get that finger in," all the restrictions that go with it. I never tell the actors what not to do, and I never tell them to do something physical. I feel that if they are not doing it, I haven't made the motion big enough to allow them to find their own place with it. I will then work toward their getting the motion bigger and then let it get smaller by itself.

CHASE: The first time I taught a five-year-old, part of the lesson was given over to her dancing, with me improvising the music for her. She would choose what she wanted to dance about—and that might even be a flower opening its pedals as the sun rose—any idea she had we used. I felt that this was very good in helping her integrate movement with making music, and developing responsiveness in a way that was natural for her.

PREVOTS-WALLEN: You are integrating all the time. If you don't think of dance as steps, and art as formalized entity, they are integrated. You are always dealing with space, time and force. The moment you sit down at the piano or take your violin you are moving. I don't care what you do, you are moving, you are painting, and actually, when you think about it, it's not just interrelating the arts as they are interrelated. You don't have to make an arbitrary interrelationship. You don't have to say, "O.K., today we are going to interrelate the arts." When you are sitting at the piano you are moving, you are making a dance. So that the instrumentalist is making music and dance and painting.

CHASE: And acting as well because the character of the music has to be acted out in music.

PREVOTS-WALLEN: That's right. And I think that musicians may be the worst offenders in isolating music from everything else. I don't know why, but they tend to be very narrow. Actors and dancers tend to be more open-ended.

CHASE: Why is that? Is it because actors and dancers are not involved in doing this through another instrument? They are their own instruments?

PREVOTS-WALLEN: Maybe that's it. . . . And . . . a musician doesn't necessarily have to relate to a director or a choreographer. . . . Improvisation seems to get a bad name. I think it has an image in people's minds of incredibly wild free-form activity and that is so unfortunate.

GLEASON: For many years I was opposed to any kind of improvisation, particularly for the training of actors because it doesn't teach you how to act. The great teachers of improvisation became directors and writers. Yoga doesn't teach you how to act, and dance doesn't teach you to act but they influence your acting enormously.

CHASE: Because they integrate these processes that you direct toward the acting or the playing. When you relate it to performance you know the free feeling you can have and you seek it, that quality, spontaneity and everything else, the natural feeling. When you know that there are such feelings to be had, then when you are working something out you are seeking to relate it to that experience, to be able to play the most intricate thing with that ease, and this is a very good guide.

PREVOTS-WALLEN: It's a tool and a process. Improvisation is not necessarily going to teach you how to get an *arabesque* or a *coupé*, but it gives you an insight and a freedom.

GLEASON: It teaches you. It's an actual technique of falling. Acting says know what you are doing. Piano playing, everything in the world says know what you are doing. There is a place for that but it is also end-gaining. Improvisation makes knowing what you are doing sensible. There isn't anything worse than someone who knows what he is doing and is not open to anything around him. Such a person isn't open to any kind of input, and so they only do what they know and it's limited to this and it's also dangerous.

PREVOTS-WALLEN: Everyone really improvises—a kid sitting down to play, even with a rigid approach is improvising, how to hold their hands. What you are saying is simply, look we all do it, recognize this and use it. Everything we do is improvising, shall I sit here, shall I sit there. How should I sit? We are always improvising and don't recognize it and sometimes don't want to because it has a bad connotation.

CHASE: You come into a room, you sit down or walk around . . .

PREVOTS-WALLEN: Even how you do that is improvising. . . . What we are saying is that improvisation is a lifelong process, you are always having to understand the connections, and in a sense a disservice is being done to young people when they are only taught as in some places, ten minutes of acrobatics, ten minutes of jazz, ten minutes of modern and some ballet and then they are considered ready. That is the biggest bit of nonsense and any child who is being taught only to play those notes is being done the same disservice that the more mature artist is being done. It is a continuous lifelong process and if they don't get it in the beginning they are really in trouble. You see this in any teaching in any school situation. The teacher who is able to interact and have that child interact with the material is getting a lifelong process started. You are not talking just about music. You don't want to eliminate the possibility of training a musician and having them develop in the best possible way, but if you don't do some of this with them you are eliminating

an important foundation. And that is a misunder-
standing. Somebody else says, "Well, they're wasting
time."

CHASE: They are learning more than that. In fact, with so
much of the contemporary composition that is aleatory, I
have heard of musicians feeling the need to get a drink before going out on stage to do this, it was so unnerving for
them to do their own improvisation in public. . . .

PREVOTS-WALLEN: There are ways of sneaking into this,
not telling people ahead of time. You end up not telling
someone to be creative, so that they can't think, "Oh no,
I don't want to be creative." There was a ballet that was
being done recently, and the ballerina, a very accomplished star was to do some improvisation, and even
though she was a choreographer, it was a most difficult
situation. Ballanchine, who was not an improvisor, from
the accounts of how he worked, would come into the
studio with no preconceived idea. He knew the music
backwards and forwards, and was a composer himself.
He would work with the individual or the couple and
say, "Now this is what I want, try it, make it work for
you." No one would think of Ballanchine as an improvisor yet he, in fact, was improvising all the time.

GLEASON: In one of Ballanchine's ballets, there is a motion that originated when he was in the studio, where
there were very large windows with the sun streaming
through. A girl who was unable to see clearly what he
was doing held up one hand stretched above her eyes. He
noticed this movement . . . and put it in the ballet; because he understood movement so thoroughly, he guided
that movement into the dance.

PREVOTS-WALLEN: I think that every good training includes some of that kind of openness. In America, we don't seem to find enough time for training people in this way. So many students rush in to take their lesson and then go on their way to something else. These things take time, there is no question about it, but they give back much for the time they take. We are a nation of instant success. Your book on improvisation will most likely be picked up mainly by music people. Dance and art and theater are not mysterious. We are in some sense always dancing, in some sense always acting, and in some sense always painting. Our own writing is our own personal expression, our own way of painting. The way we sit down or move across the room is our own way of dancing. You are using these art forms all the time but you are not aware of it.

CHASE: The way we are both talking now, we are both improvising.

PREVOTS-WALLEN: I'm moving, you're moving; I'm dancing, you're dancing; we create a dance of gesture between us. You move your body, I move mine.

CHASE: Yes, and if you were a very rigid person who moved very little . . .

PREVOTS-WALLEN: That would be my dance too, that would be my dance . . .

CHASE: And then I probably would not move . . .

PREVOTS-WALLEN: You would create your dance in relationship to that. . . .

The conversation continued, but it was this last ex-
change that remained in my mind. For some time after-
ward a consciousness of the element of improvisation in
everything we do influenced my experience of living moments, making them seem as though they moved on into
one another as though highlighted in a theater. Listening and observing, seeing and feeling the essence of
dance in all movement, transformed and added meaning
to each action, casting a glow on the act of living itself.

BIBLIOGRAPHY

Bach, C. P. E. *Essay on the True Art of Playing Keyboard Instruments.* Trans. and ed. by William J. Mitchell. New York: W. W. Norton, 1949.

Bailey, Derek. *Musical Improvisation: Its Nature and Practice in Music.* Englewood Cliffs, N.J.: Prentice-Hall, 1980.

Biasini, Americole, and Lenore Pogonowski. *Manhattanville Music Curriculum Program (MMCP) Interaction: Early Childhood Music Curriculum.* Bellingham, Wash.: available through 2101 Ontario St., Bellingham, Wash. 98225, 1979.

Cardew, Cornelius, ed. *Scratch Music.* London: Latimer New Directions, 1972.

Chang, Chung-yuan. *Creativity and Taoism: A Study of Chinese Philosophy, Art, and Poetry.* New York: Harper and Row, Colophon Books, 1970.

Chernoff, John Miller. *African Rhythm and African Sensibility.* Chicago: University of Chicago Press, 1979.

Coker, Jerry. *Improvising Jazz.* Englewood Cliffs, N.J.: Prentice-Hall, 1964.

Cone, Edward T. *The Composer's Voice*. Berkeley: University of California Press, 1974.

Copland, Aaron. *The New Music*. New York: W. W. Norton, 1968.

Czerny, Carl. *A Systematic Introduction to Improvisation on the Pianoforte*. Trans. and ed. by Alice Mitchell. New York: Longman, 1983.

Dart, Thurston. *The Interpretation of Music*. New York: Harper and Row, 1963.

Dewey, John. *Art As Experience*. New York: Capricorn Books, 1958.

Dimnet, Ernest. *The Art of Thinking*. New York: Simon and Schuster, 1929.

Firknees, Gertrude. *Klavierschule*. Zurich: Moseler Verlag, n.d.

Gelb, Michael. *Body Learning: An Introduction to the Alexander Technique*. New York: Delilah Books, 1981; distributed by Putnam.

Griffiths, Paul. *A Concise History of Avant-Garde Music*. New York: Oxford University Press, 1978.

———. *New Sounds, New Personalities: British Composers of the 1980s in Conversation with Paul Griffiths*. London: Faber Music, 1985.

Guggenheimer, Richard. *Creative Vision in Artist and Audience*. New York: Harper, 1950.

Hentoff, Nat. *Jazz Is*. New York: Limelight Editions, 1984.

Hull, S. Loraine. *Strasberg's Method as Taught by Lorrie Hull*. Woodridge, Conn.: Ox Bow Publishing, Inc., 1985.

Humphrey, Doris. *The Art of Making Dances*. New York: Grove Press, 1962.

Hutchinson, Eliot D. *How to Think Creatively*. New York: Abingdon-Cokesbury Press, 1949.

Ives, Charles. *Essays Before a Sonata.* New York: W. W. Norton, 1970.

James, William. *Psychology.* New York: H. Holt and Co., 1908.

Johnson, Tom. *Imaginary Music.* New York: Two-Eighteen Press, 1974.

Kohut, Daniel L. *Musical Performance: Learning Theory of Pedagogy.* Englewood Cliffs, N.J.: Prentice-Hall, 1985.

Maisel, Edward, ed. *The Alexander Technique: The Resurrection of the Body.* New York: University Books, 1969.

McAllester, David. "Becoming Human Through Music." In *The Wesleyan Symposium on the Perspectives of Social Anthropology in the Teaching and Learning of Music.* Reston, Va.: Music Educator's National Conference, 1985.

McMullen, Roy. *Art, Affluence, and Alienation.* New York: New American Library (Mentor Books), 1969.

Meyer, Leonard B. *Music, the Arts, and Ideas.* Chicago: University of Chicago Press, 1967.

Morgenstern, Sam, ed. *Composers on Music: An Anthology of Composer's Writings From Palestrina to Copland.* New York: Pantheon Books, 1956.

Newman, Barbara. *Striking a Balance: Dancers Talk About Dancing.* Boston: Houghton Mifflin Co., 1982.

Orff, Carl, and Gunild Keetman. *Music For Children.* (English version adapted from *Orff-Schulwerk* by Margaret Murray), 5 vols. London and Mainz: Schott, 1974.

Oyens, Tera de Marez. *Werken Mit Moderne Klanken.* Haarlem, The Netherlands: de Toorts, 1978.

Partch, Harry. *Genesis of a Music.* New York: Da Capo Press, 1979.

Rudhyar, Dane. *The Magic of Tone and the Art of Music.* Boulder, Colo.: Shambhala, 1982, dist. in U.S. by Random House.

Sachs, Curt. *The Wellsprings of Music*. New York: McGraw Hill, 1961.

Schoenberg, Arnold. *Style and Idea*. New York: Philosophical Library, 1950.

Schuller, Gunther. *The History of Jazz*. New York: Oxford University Press, 1968.

Sessions, Roger. *The Musical Experience of Composer, Performer, Listener*. Princeton: Princeton University Press, 1950.

——. *Questions About Music*. New York: W. W. Norton, 1971.

Small, Christopher. *Music, Society, Education*. New York: Schirmer, 1977.

Sorrell, Neil, and Ram Narayan. *Indian Music in Performance: A Practical Introduction*. New York: New York University Press, 1980.

Stravinsky, Igor. *Poetics of Music*. Cambridge, Mass.: Harvard University Press, 1979.

——. *Themes and Conclusions*. London: Faber, 1972.

Stravinsky, Igor, and Robert Craft. *Expositions and Developments*. Garden City, N.Y.: Doubleday, 1962.

Yates, Peter. *Twentieth Century Music*. New York: Pantheon Books, 1967.

Zemke, Lorna. *The Kodály Concept: Its History, Philosophy, and Development*. Champaign, Ill.: M. Foster Music Co., 1977.

Zuckerkandl, Victor. *Man the Musician*. Princeton: Princeton University Press, 1976.

——. *Sound and Symbol: Music and the External World*. Princeton: Princeton University Press, 1973.

About the Author

MILDRED PORTNEY CHASE began to play the piano by ear before she could speak. Her first memories of being at the piano are in her aunt's living room, picking out the melodies of songs her aunts and uncles sang. She began study at the age of five and had her own radio program at thirteen. Granted a four-year fellowship, she went on to Juilliard, where she studied with Josef Lhevinne. Later, she was featured by Peter Yates in his *Evenings on the Roof* concert series.

In recent years, the author has taught at the Los Angeles Conservatory and at the University of Southern California. Now teaching privately, she has worked with children, adult beginners, and professional musicians. *Improvisation* is her second book. *Just Being At The Piano*, her first book, was originally published by Peace Press and reissued by Creative Arts Book Company in 1985.